BELONGING

BELONGING

Betty Barnes

ATHENA PRESS
LONDON

BELONGING
Copyright © Betty Barnes 2007

All Rights Reserved

No part of this book may be reproduced in any form
by photocopying or by any electronic or mechanical means,
including information storage or retrieval systems,
without permission in writing from both the copyright
owner and the publisher of this book.

ISBN 10-digit: 1 84401 891 1
ISBN 13-digit: 978 1 84401 891 8

First Published 2007 by
ATHENA PRESS
Queen's House, 2 Holly Road
Twickenham TW1 4EG
United Kingdom

Printed for Athena Press

*For my family who make every day of the year a
'Mother's Day' for me.*

Chapter 1

My memory begins in the early 1930s in the Yorkshire spa town of Ilkley. Our house was behind my parents' ironmongery shop. There was a large back garden where I and my sister Margaret, who was two years younger than me, played and ran to the gate whenever a train chugged across the embankment high above our road. We waved to the engine drivers and they always waved back.

My dad often took me to the station to watch the trains; he had once been a railway porter so he enjoyed the bustle of arrival and departure. But I was terrified when the great juggernauts came thundering into the station, shaking the platform and hissing steam when they stopped.

Despite my fear, I never missed going to the station. I couldn't bear to be parted from my dad, so wherever he went I went too. On Sunday mornings, we went to the Baptist church where Dad was a deacon and lay preacher. He also taught the young men's class in the Sunday school. I didn't understand the church service, but I enjoyed Sunday school where we put our collection pennies in a glass jar and marched round the room singing:

> 'Hear the pennies dropping, listen while they fall,
> Everyone for Jesus, He shall have them all.'

Dad always took Margaret and me for a walk after Sunday school. In spring we went to see the bluebells in Middleton Woods and in winter, when the Tarn had frozen, we went to watch the skaters.

On weekdays, after we'd had our dinner, Dad sat us on his knees and held us spellbound with his wonderful stories. He used different voices for the characters and made us shiver with delicious terror at the booming of the 'fee fie foh fum' giant.

Mother had very little to do with me; she mostly looked after Margaret and only touched me to smack my bottom when I was naughty. From the cold way in which she looked at me, I sensed that Mother didn't like me, so I clung to Dad, who was mild-eyed, loving and gentle.

One morning he took me to the station, but we didn't go in to watch the trains. Outside the entrance, a red bus was panting to be off and reeking of petrol. Years later, the sound and smell of an old country bus could still fill me with the terror and desolation I felt on the first day I went to school.

Dad swung me up onto the bus and called, 'Here she is, Mr Crossley.' A huge man with a red face and a moustache swept me onto his knee. The bus started to move. Dad waved from the pavement, saying 'Be a good girl.' I struggled and screamed, but Mr Crossley gripped me firmly. He laughed jovially as the bus moved away.

I had been told that I was to go to school, but I had not realised that I would be separated from my dad. At first I always arrived in tears, but eventually I settled down and began to enjoy the lessons; though I was afraid of Mr Crossley, who turned out to be the headmaster.

One day he carried a screaming child into our classroom. 'Look at this cry-baby, children,' he jeered. We all laughed; we knew it was expected of us. But we didn't laugh when he caned Morton Weiss.

Each morning, before our scripture lesson started, Morton was sent to sit in the cloakroom. I was sorry for him because he missed the lovely stories about Jesus told by our teacher, Miss Shepherd. I couldn't understand why Morton should be left out of something greatly enjoyed by the rest of us, so, every playtime, Morton and I sat on a fallen tree trunk on the grass patch at the bottom of the yard and I told him the Jesus stories. He listened with solemn interest.

I had no idea that Morton was a Jewish child; I thought that the Jews had lived in biblical times. Nor did I know that I was unwittingly undermining the arrangements made to ensure Morton's exclusion from Christian instruction.

One morning, during our scripture lesson, we heard Mr Crossley shouting in the corridor. He burst into our classroom, dragging Morton by his hair; he twisted and howled as Mr Crossley hauled and jerked. 'This boy is a thief!' he bellowed. 'I caught him stealing from coat pockets in the cloakroom! Now boys and girls, I am going to teach this thieving hand a lesson.' He snatched a ruler from Miss Shepherd's desk, seized Morton's hand and hammered his skinny little knuckles. Morton screamed and writhed and tried to protect his knuckles from the red-hot agony with his other hand, but it too was belaboured. By the time it was over, we were all in tears and I had wet my knickers.

I wonder now: was six-year-old Morton really a thief? I doubt it. It is more likely that an investigation of coat pockets had relieved the lonely boredom of his banishment.

Although Mr Crossley was terrifying, he ran a very good school. Jane Austen would have thoroughly approved of his encouragement of 'the habit of early reading'. Each Friday afternoon we were permitted to take home a book from a selection set out on a table. Children whose behaviour had been excellent throughout the week were given first choice, so it was worth being good. My choice was based on size rather than content. When my name was called, I ran to the table, seized the largest book and carried it away in triumph.

However, it must be said that my behaviour did not always merit reward, either at school or at home. I remember getting into trouble on two occasions: both were to do with parties.

Not long before Christmas, I heard some of my classmates talking about the Buff's Christmas Party. I had no idea who the Buff was, but I certainly was not going to be left out of his party, which sounded wonderful, with ice cream, jelly, crackers and presents from Father Christmas.

One afternoon, just before home time, Mr Crossley came into our classroom and announced that the bus had come for the Buff children. (Their fathers must have served with the Yorkshire Buffs, an army regiment, in the 1914–1918 war). I climbed aboard with the others and off we went, leaving behind all the envious children who were not going to the party.

We were taken to a room in which animal heads were mounted on the walls. I was riveted by their glassy staring eyes. Then a bell tinkled and a voice somewhere above me called, 'Does anyone know who this little girl is?'

Somebody must have known. A tall man took me home in a car. Dad had been out looking for me and came in just as we arrived. He was very relieved to see me safe, but cross with me for causing trouble.

The tall man – I thought he must be the Buff – said, 'Bless her, she's only a bairn; she just wanted to go with her friends to the party. Why not let her come back with me? I'll bring her home later.' But the Buff left without me.

'I'll give you a party, lady,' Mother said, as she thumped me up the stairs to bed.

But I soon forgot my disgrace. One day I was invited to a classmate's birthday party. I had a great time with lots of lovely things to eat, so, when my birthday came near, I decided that I was going to have a party. I invited everyone in my class and my popularity rating soared with my promises of pink ice cream and a chocolate birthday cake.

Despite a doubtful niggle at the back of my mind (parties were unheard of in our house), I convinced myself that Mother was going to say, 'Oh, it's your birthday on Saturday! You must have a party.' By the time Thursday came and she hadn't said a word, the niggle was beginning to grow. But I told myself there was still time, and anyway she hadn't said I couldn't have a party. I ignored the fact that I had not given her the opportunity to refuse. When Saturday came, I knew that all was lost. After our midday dinner, I sat trying to read my birthday book, but my eyes kept going to the clock on the mantelpiece. All I could think of was the trouble I was going to be in when my classmates turned up at three o'clock. Mother was absorbed in her knitting; Dad was reading his newspaper. Their peaceful ignorance of what was about to happen made me feel even worse. I wished I wasn't me, but somebody else, a long way off.

At long last the clock struck the hour of my doom and there was a knock at the back door. Dad put his paper aside and went to the door. I sat quailing until he came back, alone.

Mother paused from counting stitches. 'Who was it?'

Dad looked hard at me. 'It was a little girl. She said, "Please, Sir, I'm Una. I've come to Betty's party."'

'Party! What party?' Mother demanded. 'I never said you could have a party.'

'Did you invite anyone else?' Dad asked worriedly.

'Only Una,' I lied. I daren't admit that I'd asked my entire class.

Fortunately for me, no one else came – no doubt that was because parents had not received the customary formal invitation – but I got a stern lecture from Dad. He said that Una had probably gone home crying because she had been looking forward to a party, so what I had done was very unkind.

To this day I wonder whether Una did cry on her way home. But most of all I wonder why, if only for her sake, we couldn't have had a bit of a party. After all, how long does it take to knock up a few buns and nip out for some ice cream?

But Una was turned away. Was that kind? I don't think so. But to be fair, it was probably just a thoughtless reaction to an unexpected situation.

One of the best things I remember was the arrival of a young girl who lived with us and did the housework. Margaret and I loved cheerful Gladys and she always had time for us. I slept with her in the attic and her comforting presence stopped me having nightmares. Dad was pleased; he had often got out of bed and run to me when I woke up screaming.

Mother wasn't all that keen on Gladys and constantly found fault with her house cleaning. I knew that Mother was very particular. Before Gladys came I had been given the job of dusting the stairs because, Mother said, I spent far too much time with my 'nose stuck in a book'. Each of the knobbly rails beneath the banister had to be carefully wiped so that Mother's inspecting finger would find not a speck of dust. There were three flights of stairs up to the attic, so it was a long, boring job. But after Gladys came, she showed me how to do it in no time: I just ran up and down the stairs, swiping my duster at the rails as I flew past. When Mother caught me swipe dusting, she gave me what for. I didn't tell on Gladys, but Mother had no doubt whose idea it was. She said that she wasn't having Gladys teaching me her lazy ways.

She said the same thing about another of Gladys's time-saving customs. I had noticed that, when Gladys came to bed, she took off her frock and put her nightdress on over the rest of her clothes. When I asked why she didn't undress to her skin as I did, she said there was no point in taking all your clothes off when you had to put them back on again next morning.

This seemed entirely logical to me, but not to Mother when she came up to the attic one morning to waken

Gladys, who'd overslept, and found me wearing my nightdress over my clothes. We both got a lecture about 'sluttish habits'. Gladys didn't care, so I didn't either. After Mother had gone we had a good giggle, so I knew that Gladys and I were allies.

Whilst Gladys was a ray of sunshine in our house, it wasn't long before a black cloud arrived in the shape of Nurse Paget. Suddenly the house seemed to be filled with her starch-crackling presence. Margaret and I were afraid of her, so we kept out of her way as she marched grimly up and down the stairs with trays for Mother, who was mysteriously in bed, even though it was daytime.

We clung to Gladys in the kitchen; we felt safe with her. We knew that she would protect us and indeed she did, when Nurse Paget lost her silver thimble and accused Margaret and me of hiding it, although we had done no such thing.

'They haven't touched your bloomin' thimble,' Gladys told her. 'Crabby old moustache face!' she muttered, as Nurse Paget took her baleful glare out of the kitchen.

'Why has Nurse Paget got a moustache?' Margaret asked.

Gladys grinned wickedly. 'Why don't you ask her?'

So Margaret did. We were all having our tea, but it was a silent meal. Nurse Paget's presence froze all communication apart from a polite, 'More tea, Nurse?' from Dad.

Suddenly Margaret piped up, 'Nurse Paget, why have you got a moustache?'

'Margaret!' Dad exclaimed in horror.

Gladys spluttered into her teacup and I made things worse. 'But, Dad, only men have moustaches so why—?'

'That will do.' He turned to Nurse Paget. 'I'm sorry my little girls are so rude.'

She folded her lips in a tight line and nodded meaningfully at us; so we knew that we hadn't heard the last of it. But she bided her time.

The next day we actually saw her smiling, so we weren't afraid of what she might do to us when she beckoned us to follow her upstairs. 'I've got a surprise for you,' she said. 'Wait there.' Then she went into Mother's bedroom and came back with a shawl-wrapped bundle. 'Look!' She pulled aside the shawl and we gazed at a tiny face.

'Is it a doll?' I asked uncertainly.

'Doll! It's your new baby sister.'

We went downstairs to Gladys. She beamed at us. 'Well, what did you think of the surprise?'

'It was only a baby,' I told her.

She was amazed. 'Don't you like babies?'

'I'd rather have a puppy,' Margaret said mournfully, and I agreed.

It is strange now to reflect that, for us, the arrival of the new baby, Edwina, was almost a non-event. But in those days parents seldom prepared their children for an addition to the family, so, for us, there had been no anticipation of the event leading to a joyful welcome when the baby arrived.

To Margaret and me, the baby was just a nuisance, because Nurse Paget was always hissing at us, 'Stop making all that noise, you'll waken Baby.' It seemed to us that the baby had changed everything, and not for the better.

One day Nurse Paget announced that she was taking the baby on her first outing, so Margaret and I were to go too. It was freezing outside, so Gladys put our legs in leather gaiters; they were like long stockings but with many buttons up the sides.

We set off with Nurse Paget in her outdoor uniform, topped by a dark blue veil floating behind her. Margaret and I clung to the sides of the pram. We scuttled along as fast as we could, but we couldn't keep up with Nurse Paget as she marched swiftly along the icy path by the river. Our feet were slipping and sliding as we were dragged along, hanging on to the pram and whimpering with fear. Suddenly we skidded and let go of the pram. Nurse Paget swept on, leaving us terrified and marooned on a patch of ice. We both began to bawl and people walking by the river turned to see what all the noise was about. The sight of a uniformed nurse abandoning her screaming charges on the ice must have caused raised eyebrows; she stopped and came back for us.

We continued along the path at a much slower pace. It began to snow, so we sheltered under a railway bridge until we had to go because it was time for 'Baby's feed'.

We arrived home coated with snow. Much to our surprise Nurse Paget bustled us straight into a hot bath. 'Why are we having a bath in the middle of the day?' I demanded.

'To warm you up, then you won't get a cold.' She got to work on our skin with a rough loofah.

We laughed at the absurd idea that we could we get a cold just because a bit of snow had fallen on us. But we stopped laughing when she made us get into bed. This was too much; bedtime was hours away and we hadn't been naughty.

We wailed in protest as Nurse Paget bandaged us into our beds with tightly tucked sheets. 'Why must we stay in bed?' howled Margaret.

'Germs, that's why. If you have caught a cold, we can't risk you giving it to Baby.'

I was fed up with the baby. This was all her fault. 'I hate the baby,' I yelled.

'Temper!' Nurse Paget nodded knowingly. 'System's out of order. I'll soon fix that.'

She fetched a bottle of medicine and dosed me. 'What is it?' I asked after I'd swallowed the second vile tasting spoonful.

'Castor oil.' She put the cork back in the bottle with a smart tap.

'Mm, it's lovely,' I lied. 'What's it for?'

'You'll see.' And indeed I did. I spent the rest of the day

running to the toilet, which no doubt afforded Nurse Paget much grim satisfaction. One way or another, she'd certainly got her own back for the moustache episode.

When she left a few days later, Margaret and I danced for joy. 'She's gone! She's gone!' we exulted. Little did we know that we had not seen the last of Nurse Paget.

Dad always put me to bed and said prayers with me. One night, after we'd God-blessed everyone, he said, 'Guess who's coming tomorrow.'

I bounced up in bed and cried, 'Uncle Lennie!' After Dad had gone downstairs, I lay hugging myself with delight because Uncle was coming. He was one of Dad's brothers; later I was to meet more uncles, but Uncle Lennie was always to come first with me. I adored him.

The next morning seemed to pass very slowly, but at last there he was, standing in the living room doorway just as I remembered him, with his red-gold hair, twinkling blue eyes and beaming smile. 'Hello, love. Have you got a kiss for me?'

I leapt up into his arms. We all sat down to dinner but I was too excited to eat and Mother said her usual bit about starving children who would be grateful for my leavings.

Uncle nudged me. 'You're too glad to eat, aren't you, love?' How well he knew that my cup of joy was so full that I had no room for rice pudding. 'Tell you what,' he said, 'this afternoon we'll have a treat. I'll take you out to tea in a café.' Mother was not pleased about that, but I was over the moon; I had never been to a café.

First we went to the river, where Uncle showed me how to skim stones and make them bounce across the water. Then we went to the Bluebird Café, where I had often admired three beautiful bluebirds flying across the gleaming white frontage. We were just about to go in when a voice exclaimed, 'Well! Fancy seeing you, Lennie!' When I looked round, Uncle was shaking hands with two young ladies. To my dismay he invited them to take tea with us.

We sat at a window table and ate boiled eggs, brown bread and cream cakes. But my treat was spoiled by those silly, giggling females, who were taking Uncle's attention away from me. He was telling them jokes that I couldn't understand and they kept tittering, 'Oh! Lennie, you cheeky thing!'

Then one of them – she wore a horrible hat like an upturned plant pot – said, 'Still not married, Lennie?'

'Nobody will have me,' he chuckled.

I sensed that both ladies wanted him and I was furiously jealous; Uncle was mine. I sat scowling until he switched his attention to me. The ladies took their cue from him, 'What a dear little girl. What heavenly eyes!' But I refused to be drawn. When Uncle wasn't looking, I stuck out my tongue at the interlopers. Horrible-hat promptly crossed her eyes and stuck out her tongue at me. I was stunned; I had never imagined that a grown-up could be so rude!

The next morning Uncle had to leave. I got up early so that I wouldn't miss a moment of the little time I had left to be with him. The awful moment came. He bent down and drew me into his arms, 'Promise you won't cry when I've gone.' We both knew that I would weep buckets after the door had closed behind him, and I did.

A few months later, Dad told me that we were leaving Ilkley and going to live at Blackpool. 'It's where you were born,' he said. 'Your grandma lives there; she has a boarding house where people stay for holidays in summer.'

The reason for the move was given to me in later years. Dad feared that his side street shop was going to lose customers because another ironmongery was to be opened in Ilkley's main shopping area, so he decided to transfer his business to Blackpool, where he and Mother could enjoy being near to various relatives.

As things turned out, they would have done better to have stayed where they were: fifty years later Dad's Ilkley shop was still there, extended and thriving. But the move to Blackpool was to be the start of my parents' endless struggle to survive in business during the depression of the 1930s.

So, to Blackpool we went; but I never forgot beautiful Ilkley: the sparkling river, the glorious bluebells in Middleton Woods, the sunlit landscape below the 'Cow and Calf' rocks on the moor, and the ice-white wonderland of the Tarn on a winter day. They are all forever enshrined in my childhood memory.

Chapter 2

I had my first train ride the day we moved to Blackpool. After the removal van had gone with all our furniture, we hurried to the station; our train was about to depart as we scrambled aboard. A few minutes later we steamed across the embankment above our garden. 'Wave goodbye to our house,' Dad cried. I looked down from the carriage window and saw my doll's pram, forgotten and forlorn, tip-tilted on the garden path. I burst into howls of grief for my lost pram; but I soon forgot my woe when Dad started Margaret and me on a blot-spotting competition. In those days, every station displayed an advertisement for Stephens Ink. It featured an enormous blue blot splashed on a white background. The first to spot the blot won a toffee.

When we got near to Blackpool, Dad said, 'The first to spot the Tower wins a ha'penny.'

We had no idea what the Tower was. We gazed eagerly over the flat landscape until we saw, in the distance, something tall and slender pointing to the sky: 'The Tower!' we cried and Dad gave us both a ha'penny.

A few minutes later, the train slowed and stopped inside a station. On the platform, a man wearing a peaked cap shouted, 'Blackpool South Shore. All change!'

We didn't go straight to our new abode; we went to Grandma's boarding house on busy Lytham Road, where trams sailed past on their way to the Promenade. Grandma was plump with grey hair in a bun. She gave us a smiling welcome and hugged me. 'My bairn! How you've grown!'

Although I didn't remember her from earlier years, I somehow knew that she loved me; perhaps it was because she had called me her bairn. We had a meal of sausage and mash in the living room. It was a bit of a squash.

As well as a large table, there were various chairs, a leather couch and a massive sideboard, on which was a large bible with golden clasps – like the one in our Ilkley chapel.

I whispered to Dad, 'Why has Grandma got a chapel bible?'

He told me that it was a family bible and that all the birth and wedding dates of her family were written inside it. 'I'm in there, so are you,' he said. I wanted to see my name but Dad said that we must go to the new house because the removal van would be arriving with our furniture.

Grandma said something to Dad, then she turned to me. 'How would you like to stop with me for a bit, pet?'

My eyes went to Dad's face. 'Just till we get settled in the new house,' he said. 'You'll be all right with your grandma.'

Grandma was nodding and smiling at me; suddenly I knew that I very much wanted to stay.

As it turned out, I stayed with Grandma for several weeks. Schools had closed for the long summer break, so I was free until they reopened. It was to be a wonderful summer filled with new experiences, one of which was my first day with Grandma.

Although I was then too young to fully comprehend the sheer hard grind of a boarding house landlady's daily round in the holiday season, I can see it now.

The shrilling of an alarm clock woke me. I was in the attic where Grandma and I slept on camp beds. When all the bedrooms were full of holidaymakers (in those days called visitors), landladies and their families slept in attics and cellars.

Grandma rolled out of bed and began to dress. I watched intrigued as she laced herself into corsets and hoisted up a vast pair of bloomers.

Next came black stockings with elastic garters, then a petticoat; over this she tied a small apron with a pocket across the front. I could hear money jingling in the pocket. (Grandma only used a handbag when she went to church). The final layer included a black dress and a wraparound flowered overall. Then she sat on the bed and thrust her feet into flat-heeled shoes; they had a button on each strap, which she fastened with a buttonhook. Puffed by her exertions, she paused to get her breath back.

'Can I get up, Grandma?' I asked.

'Oh, bairn, go back to sleep. It's only half-past six.' But I was already scrambling into my clothes.

On the way downstairs, we passed bedrooms with numbers on the doors. One door had letters, WC. It was the only one in the house, so you had to get in there before the visitors formed a queue; it was the same with the single bathroom.

Our ablutions done, we descended to the kitchen. There was a sink, a wall cupboard, a table and an enormous gas stove that took up nearly all the space.

Grandma showed me how to set the tables for the visitors' breakfasts in the front room, then we sat down to bacon butties. When the visitors started clumping down the stairs, I trotted back and forth with plates of egg, bacon and fried bread, plus cups of tea. The visitors greeted my appearance with cries of, 'Hello, hinney,' and 'Who's this bonny lass?' They laughed and joked all the time; they were the happiest people that I had ever seen.

Whilst Grandma washed up and I dried, I asked her where the visitors came from. She told me, 'Spennymoor. It's in Durham. I used to live there too, so my visitors are mostly old friends and their families.' So now I knew why Grandma spoke in the same way as the visitors and why the name beside her front door was 'Spennymoor'.

The next job was shopping. We went out the back gate

into a narrow alley where two red-haired boys of about my age were playing cricket. They stopped and looked enquiringly at me. Grandma told them, 'This is your cousin Betty. She's come to stop with me for a bit.' George and Ted were to become my buddies; they were part of a family enclave consisting of three boarding houses backing onto the alley.

Grandma took me to several shops on busy Lytham Road. Our last call was at The Pudding Kitchen, where there was a washing day smell from steamers bubbling on massive stoves. Dozens of small sponge puddings were set out on trays; Grandma bought two dozen at a penny each.

When we got home, she set pans of vegetables to boil and basted an enormous joint to roast in the oven. The kitchen was like an oven. Grandma's hair escaped in wisps from her bun and clung damply to her forehead as she carved the meat and made a big jug of custard.

The visitors crowded into the front room and I sped back and forth with plates and jugs of gravy, followed by the sponge puddings topped with jam and custard, then the cups of tea without which no meal was complete.

After the visitors had been fed, Grandma and I had our dinner and I had a delicious fizzy drink called dandelion and burdock. Full of food and fizz, I could hardly move. 'Get down on the couch and shut your eyes, pet,' Grandma said. She put a cushion under my head and gave me a kiss. As I drifted off to sleep, I heard her start on the washing up. When I woke up, she had just finished and begun to cut the bread for the visitors' tea (there was no sliced bread then). I buttered dozens of slices, then Grandma showed me how to set the front room tables with boiled ham and tomatoes, glass dishes of tinned fruit with Fussel's tinned cream, and cakes.

The window table had to have the most delectable cakes because, Grandma said, visitors coming from the station, looking for somewhere to stay, peered through windows to find a house that set a good table. Further enticement was provided by a notice in the window: 'Three knife and fork meals a day'.

The visitors came in; they seemed to spend a great deal of their time coming back from the beach etc. for meals. After tea, instead of going out again, some of them gathered round the seat in the small front garden. One of the men had an accordion. 'Come and have a sing with us, pet,' they told me. So I sat blissfully ensconced between the visitors as we sang the popular songs of the thirties, such as 'Red Sails in the Sunset' and 'When I Grow Too Old to Dream, I'll Have You to Remember'.

Trams sailed by like tall lit-up ships in the gathering dusk; the visitors bought fish and chips from the shop across the road and generously shared their supper with me. My happiness was complete. I decided that, when I grew up, I was going to be a visitor and have a wonderful life, just like these happy laughing people.

I ran indoors to tell Grandma that I was going to be a visitor. She was sitting down at last, but she wasn't resting. She was peeling potatoes for the next day's dinner. 'Oh, bairn!' she exclaimed. 'It's long past your bedtime.'

Tired out though she must have been, she puffed all the way up to the attic to tuck me in and give me a loving goodnight kiss, before going downstairs again to finish her tasks. I lay drowsy and content. When the luminous green fingers of the alarm clock pointed to midnight, Grandma, her gruelling day over at last, flopped wearily into bed.

The next day, a young girl came from Spennymoor to help Grandma. With Vera's arrival, Grandma didn't need my help, so I was able to go with my cousins, George and Ted, who wanted to show me around Blackpool.

I well remember our first outing, when they showed me how you could enjoy the delights of Blackpool without spending a penny. As it happened I was not penniless because, before we set off, Grandma delved in the money pocket beneath her skirt and gave me three pennies – riches to me, as I'd never had more than one.

We went to the Promenade, where I caught a brief glimpse of the sea before we were swallowed up by the crowds thronging the Golden Mile with its amusement arcades and shows.

My pennies were burning a hole in my pocket, so when we came to a booth offering 'astounding wonders' such as the king of the London sewer rats and the sheep with six legs, all for three pence, I wanted to go in. But Ted told me, 'Don't waste your money on that. The rat isn't a rat, it's a coypu, and the sheep hasn't got six legs, the extras are just little stumps like sausages.'

Seeing my disappointment, George said, 'Come on, we'll go and see Crippen hanged; you'll like that.'

We went into a slot machine arcade and stopped in front of a glass-fronted miniature theatre, in which the grizzly spectacle of Crippen's execution could be enjoyed for a penny. The boys waved away my offer of the penny and said that we didn't need to pay. They were right. A man wearing a 'kiss me quick' hat appeared. 'Want to see Crippen gettin' 'is neck stretched, kids?' He put a penny in the slot. There was a whirring sound, then double doors began to open on illuminated scenes.

First we saw Crippen standing in the dock before a judge with a black square over his wig. The doors closed and another scene opened to reveal Crippen kneeling before a man in a white dog collar who was holding a bible. 'Sayin' 'is prayers afore they top 'im,' kiss me quick said with relish. In the final scene, Crippen was standing on a trap door. There was a bag over his head and a rope tied to a beam was round his neck. A man beside him pulled a lever; the trapdoor opened and Crippen crashed down with a clang. The doors closed but they didn't quite shut, so I could still see the dangling rope. There was a whirr and Crippen came up to stand again on the trap door. With a final buzz, the doors shut tight.

We left the arcade and made our way past stalls selling shrimps, buckets, spades, flags for sandcastles and colourful windmills whirling gaily in the breeze. Ahead was Blackpool Tower. I could see a lift going up inside the mesh of iron girders. 'Are we going up there?' I asked nervously. I hoped not; it looked so terribly high up.

Much to my relief George said, 'No, we're going to show you how they make Blackpool rock.'

A demonstration was just about to start as we wormed our way to the front of the crowd in the rock shop. Commanding the scene was a man in a white chef's hat. 'Right!' he cried, 'I'm goin' to show you how we make our famous Blackpool rock.' He dumped a mound of soft white rock on the counter and stretched it into a long roll which he neatly looped over a hook nailed to a post at the end of the counter. He pulled and cast the roll back and forth over the hook until its sheen was like silk.

'I wouldn't stand too close, Missis, if I was you,' he warned a stout lady standing near the hook. 'I'm not tellin' you a lie,' he went on, still throwing and pulling, 'there was a woman standin' there last week an' I missed me 'ook – right round 'er neck it went.' The crowd roared with laughter and he transferred the roll to the counter.

The rest of the demonstration revealed how letters or flowers were built into the rock with coloured strips, and then he passed round free samples. There was a beautiful violet all the way through the miniature sticks of rock that the boys and I received.

The rock chef then seized a large paper bag and flipped it open. 'Now, Missis,' he said to the stout lady, ''ow about takin' a spot of Blackpool rock back 'ome? Tell you what I'll do, I'll make you up our special two bob bag.' She smiled and nodded. He turned to the shelves full of rock. 'Two large Blackpool... four vi'lets an' four straws... 'umbugs an' lollies,' he cried as he brandished each handful aloft before thrusting it into the bulging bag. He paused, about to hand it over. 'Will you 'ave another stick if I give you one, luv?' She nodded, rocking with laughter as he crammed another stick into the bag. 'Two bob, luv. Ta. Now, who else wants one?'

A forest of hands waved two shilling coins. White coated assistants appeared carrying trays of ready made-up bags. They did a roaring trade, but I could see that those bags were nowhere near as full as the stout lady's, so I decided that if ever I had two bob to spend on rock, I would be the first customer.

We wandered away blissfully sucking our rock; it had made us very thirsty, so I volunteered my pennies to buy pop. But the boys knew where to get free drinks. They took me to a stall where a man was demonstrating fruit juice extractors to a large audience. I was getting quite good at crowd penetration, so I soon got to the front and stood between the boys. When the man had filled a jug with orange juice, he poured three glasses and handed them to the nearest children – we three of course.

'Look at that, folks,' he told the crowd. 'It's the easiest way to give your kids the vitamins they need to grow strong and healthy – and see how they love it!'

We took the hint and showed how we loved it by pausing between gulps to grin ecstatically and smack our lips. A lot of people bought extractors so we felt that we done our bit in exchange for the free drinks.

By this time we were hungry, so we ate the cold chip butties that Grandma had made with chips left over from the previous evening's meal. Then we went along the Promenade to The Pleasure Beach. In those days, exotic white and gold domes glittering in the sun drew holiday-makers towards the fun in store.

You could hear the noise from miles away, especially the

piercing high-pitched yowls of spectres haunting The Ghost Train. Shouts of barkers and stallholders mingled with screams from people hurtling up and down The Big Dipper and the roars of mechanical laughter from the King of Fun in his glass box outside The Fun House.

There were dozens of rides and all the world seemed to be plunging, spinning and whirling. Everyone was eating ice cream, waffles and wodges of pink stuff like sparkling cotton wool. Bemused by it all, I wanted to stop and gaze at everything, but the boys urged me on until we came to a booth surrounded by a noisy crowd. A barker was shouting, 'Six balls for three pence! Drop 'im in the drink!'

A man was sitting on a seat suspended above a tank full of water. Above him was a small round target at which, amidst much hilarity, men were hurling the balls.

'Garn – yer couldn't knock the skin off a rice pudding,' the man on the seat jeered as balls hit the net protecting his head and body. Suddenly a ball hit the target and the seat gave way, plunging him into the tank. He arose, dripping, glaring and shaking his fist at the cheering crowd. Without doubt, he had the worst job on The Pleasure Beach. Nobody lasted for long on the ducking seat. Some got pneumonia from sitting soaking wet from morning till midnight and some died. But many men were unemployed during the depression years, so there was always someone glad of the job.

I was told this by my Uncle Benny who, for many years, did various jobs on the Golden Mile and The Pleasure Beach. That summer he was working in The Children's Corner on the Beach where there were roundabouts and swing boats; we made our way there. Uncle was in charge of a miniature Ferris wheel on which the children rode in birdcage cabins. We watched him peeping into the revolving cages, his blue eyes twinkling in his sun-browned face, as he whistled and tweeted and said, 'Hello, my bonnie canaries, sing for Uncle Benny.'

He was delighted to see his nephews and niece and he offered us a free ride, but we would have been a tight fit in a birdcage, so, determined to treat us to something, he gave us a penny each for ice cream.

We went back to the Promenade and sat on a bench at a tram stop to eat our ice cream. I very much wanted to suggest a tram ride home; it was a long way back to Grandma's and I had got blisters burning my heels. But I was afraid that, if I moaned, the boys might think that I was a 'wet lettuce' (a current term applied to pathetic nuisances, especially girls), so I kept quiet.

Just then a tram slowed to a halt and the driver waved to us. Ted said, 'Oh, it's Uncle Jim. Come on, free ride.' We hopped on board.

I later learned that Uncle Jim Kidd, a big burly man, was an ex-footballer. Years ago, when Grandma and her family had lived in Spennymoor, Jim had played for a local team and married Grandma's eldest daughter, Jessie. After the 1914–1918 war, Jim had been signed on to play for Blackpool. So he and Jessie had arrived in Blackpool, where they had rented a boarding house to supplement Jim's pay which, in those days, was nowhere near the astronomical sums earned by the current gods of football.

At this time, Grandma, who'd had thirteen children and raised eleven without the help of her alcoholic husband, decided to leave him and make a fresh start. She and most of her family had followed Jim and Jessie to Blackpool. So that was why so many of the Gibson family were now established in Blackpool as an integral part of the resort's holiday industry.

We did indeed get a free ride on Uncle's tram. As we took our seats, he popped out of his cabin and gave us a penny each for our fares. The conductor clipped our tickets and gave us a ha'penny change.

My ha'penny, added to my still unspent three pennies,

meant that I arrived home owning more money than I'd set off with! It had been a truly wonderful day.

I was blissfully happy living with Grandma and roaming around Blackpool with my cousins, who made me feel that nothing they did was complete without me. I knew that it couldn't last because I would have to go home. At the back of my mind, there was a confused feeling about this: I wanted to see my dad, but I didn't want to go home. Sometimes, at odd moments, the feeling surfaced but I pushed it away. After all, going home hadn't happened up to now; and I was totally absorbed in my life among the family clan on Lytham Road where aunties and uncles, as well as Grandma, always made me welcome.

Much to my joy, Uncle Lennie arrived for his annual holiday. He said that he had booked a bed in Grandma's washhouse – a joking reference to the fact that although all the beds were occupied by visitors, Grandma always found room for members of her family.

Every morning, Uncle assembled his nephews and nieces round the front garden seat and outlined our plans for the day. This group included more of my cousins from adjacent boarding houses. Like me, all the cousins thought that Uncle was great. He had acquired a small car, which made him even more marvellous in our eyes (few people owned a car in those days). We would all cram in and off we'd go.

Our favourite venue – Uncle's too – was the open-air café on the top of Pablo's ice cream factory, where we had a competition to see who could eat the most ice cream. The winner was supposed to be the first one to be sick and the prize was some more ice cream. But none of us, even when we were back in the car, ever qualified for the first prize, despite generous dollops of ice cream swimming in raspberry sauce.

Another of Uncle's treats was a visit to the open-air swimming pool on the Promenade. He wore an ancient black costume spotted with moth holes; he said that he wasn't going to buy a new one because there were 'no holes anywhere important'.

We went boating on the lake in Stanley Park and had a picnic on the grass by the floral clock, followed by a session of Uncle's action songs.

We began with 'Mary Had Some Marmalade', in the course of which Mary consumed an extraordinary mixture of food with the inevitable result:

> Whoops came the marmalade and whoops came the jam,
> Whoops came the potted meat and whoops came the ham,
> Whoops came the onions and a couple of pints of beer
> And then Mary realized why she felt so queer.

You did the 'whoops' with graphic noisy gusto, as if you were being sick. We loved it best of all Uncle's songs. Before long, there would be a crowd of children sitting with us and begging for 'One Finger, One Thumb, Keep Moving', just once more.

All too soon, Uncle's holiday came to end. Sadly we waved him off as he drove away. I struggled to hold back my tears. 'What shall we do today?' George asked, as we sat disconsolately on the garden seat after Uncle had gone. But nobody answered. We knew that nothing we did now could be the same without the jovial, adventuring spirit of Uncle Lennie. With his going, the joyful merry-go-round on which I had spun all summer slowed and came to a halt. That evening Dad came to collect me.

Chapter 3

A few minutes' walk took us to 89 Ansdell Road. It was a double-fronted shop with rooms behind and above. We went in through the shop door. Much to my surprise, Dad was no longer selling ironmongery; the shop was set out with furniture and carpets. There was even a little office with a telephone and a typewriter. I wanted to have a go at typing straight away, but the shop bell rang so Dad went to serve a customer.

I opened the door to our living quarters. It was the first time, but certainly not the last, that I was to see our familiar furniture in a strange setting. It was a small room, overcrowded with our dining table and chairs. There was a fireplace range with a side oven, and a window looking out on a patch of scruffy grass and a brick wash house.

The door to the kitchen opened and Mother came in. 'Oh. So you're back, are you?' I stood stricken as her stony grey eyes looked me over. 'Your hair needs cutting,' she said accusingly.

Suddenly I realised why I hadn't wanted to come home: it was because of Mother. I had always known that she didn't like me, and her rejection of me during my Ilkley years had merely been a part of the only world that I knew. But now I had encountered a different world in which Grandma had shown me love; she had hugged and kissed me. The difference between Grandma, who loved me very much, and Mother, who didn't love me at all, hit me like a blow and I burst into tears. But later, when I lay in bed, I comforted myself with the cheering thought that Grandma was not far away, so I could often be with her.

My new school had a strange name: Revoe. On the whole I liked it. Of course it had a couple of drawbacks, but then hadn't most things. The headmistress, Miss Dobson, was one. She was imposingly large; the floor creaked beneath her elephantine tread and her booming voice could be heard all over the school when she bellowed, 'Take ten black stars!' at some terrified miscreant. She was so feared that her progress through the school was marked by victims with wet knickers.

Her domination of our lives was complete. She even dictated our bedtime, seven o'clock, and assured us that she would be carrying out evening surveillance: 'Woe betide any girl I catch on the streets!'

I certainly believed her threat so, when Mother told me to take the wireless battery to be recharged after seven o'clock, I said that I couldn't go because of Miss Dobson's curfew. 'Dobbo doesn't give the orders here,' Mother snapped, so off I went, fearfully peering round corners in case Miss Dobson should be lurking. My instinct was to run as fast as I could, but I had to go slowly; the heavy battery had to be carried very carefully because the acid it contained could spill and burn my legs.

I arrived home heartily thankful that there had been no sign of Miss Dobson. But the next day's events revealed what could happen to you if you were caught doing something even more terrible than curfew breaking.

In the school's hall a special assembly took place. It was, to quote an old naval term, 'all hands on deck to witness punishment'. Sally Langford was to be punished for playing truant. She'd had no more sense than to go playing on the swings in the park. The girls' school was on the floor above the boys' school, so Miss Dobson had the advantage of a good view of the park from the upstairs windows, from where she had spotted the truant and descended wrathfully. So now Sally stood facing Miss Dobson on the platform.

First she got a thundering dressing down, then Miss Dobson declared that such disgraceful behaviour had lowered the proud flag of our school. This was indeed a most heinous crime. 'Keep the flag of Revoe flying high!' was Miss Dobson's frequent excelsior cry, delivered with a dramatically up-flung arm and finger pointing aloft. We had all been made aware that, if we did anything to make that flying flag droop, a severe punishment would follow, so we knew that poor Sally was really for it.

'Head girl, go and ask Mr Singleton if I may borrow his cane.' The whole school stood tense and silent as the head girl's footsteps tapped down the stone stair to the boys' school. We even heard her knock on the headmaster's study door, and the murmur of voices. Then the footsteps came clocking starkly back up the stair. Every eye was riveted on the cane as the head girl carried it through our petrified ranks to the platform.

Miss Dobson took the cane. 'Hand!' she demanded. Sally flung out her right hand sideways. Miss Dobson adjusted the hand to shoulder level with the tip of the cane and gave Sally's palm a stinging cut. She flinched and her mouth gaped in pain. 'Hand!' Miss Dobson said again. The cane smote Sally's left hand and the girl standing next to me threw up all over the floor.

Corporal punishment was administered in most school schools then, but I never saw anything more terrifying than that morning's performance. It wasn't just the caning – two strokes was lenient for those days. What really left its impression on all of us was that appalling wait in absolute silence, with tension building for what seemed like ages, whilst we waited for the instrument of punishment to be fetched. Of course that theatrical orchestration of waiting was the real, never to be forgotten, deterrent to misdoing, which no doubt was Miss Dobson's intention.

Although she was a stern disciplinarian, it is only fair to say that she loved and lived for her school. The high standards that she set for hard work, good behaviour and cleanliness were for our good as well as to maintain the reputation of the school. But, when it came to cleanliness, she went too far.

She had it in for any girl who appeared at school scruffy or unwashed. She told us, 'You can keep yourself clean even if you live on Ibbison Street.' I could hardly believe that she could say such a thing when several girls, including Mary in my class, lived on Ibbison Street (it was known as the town's slum). Poor Mary, well aware that we knew where she lived, hung her head in shame at this public reference to her home conditions.

The best thing about Revoe as far as I was concerned was being in Miss Higham's class. She loved teaching, so she made us share her enthusiasm for the subjects that she taught. At the end of each day she read to us an excerpt from a book. She said that, if we wanted to hear more, we must get the book from the public library. The librarian was surprised but gratified when almost the whole of our class became first-time borrowers. Apart from one short period, when my ticket was confiscated by Dad, I have never been without a well-used ticket from that day to this.

One day, Miss Higham had us all laughing at the comedy of the waiter who ate most of David Copperfield's dinner at the inn. Suddenly the door opened and Miss Dobson tramped in. She glared round and announced that we had a thief in our midst. A girl in our class had reported the disappearance of a ha'penny from her desk.

Miss Dobson made us all stand on our desk seats, then she came round and ran her finger inside the elastic of our knicker-legs. No ha'penny emerged, but she gave us a stern lecture on honesty that made us all feel guilty of the theft. Then, having cast blight on our normally happy classroom, she departed.

I looked at Miss Higham; her usually smiling face was taut, so I knew that she didn't like Miss Dobson's treatment of her class. But our spirits were soon restored. Miss Higham went to the cupboard and took out the wind-up gramophone; we were soon enjoying a session of country dancing. The dances had lovely names: Gathering Peascods, Bobeep and Sellenger's Round. We had to perform them perfectly because we were to compete in the Folk Dance section at the annual music festival in the Winter Gardens. We did, in fact, keep the flag of Revoe flying high by winning the cup. Miss Dobson lauded our success at assembly, so we were in her good books. Not that I cared about that; I cared only for Miss Higham. I sensed that she liked me, and I adored her, so I did everything I could to gain her approval.

As well as enjoying school, I had Saturdays to look forward to when I went to sit with Grandma. The summer season was over; all the visitors had gone, so there were lean months ahead for residents whose annual incomes were dependent on the holiday season. This state of affairs had given Blackpool its reputation for 'three months hard labour and nine months starvation'.

People had to find a way to survive until the visitors returned. Grandma earned a little money by making quilts, which she sold to market stall proprietors. Girls in Grandma's youth in Durham had been taught quilt making by their mothers.

One Saturday afternoon I sat watching Grandma at work on a pink satin quilt stretched on a frame. I loved those afternoons, when I had Grandma all to myself and we sat cosily by the fire. We didn't talk much, but for me it was enough to be there, secure in the warmth of Grandma's loving welcome.

After a while I looked at the clock on the sideboard to see if it was nearly teatime; I was beginning to feel hungry. My eye was caught by Grandma's bible. I remembered that Dad had told me it was a family bible with my name inside it, so now I asked, 'Can I look in your bible, Grandma?'

She pushed her glasses up her nose and looked at me. 'No, pet,' she said gently but firmly. 'There's something in there that you mustn't know until you are older.' I recollect quite clearly that those were her exact words. Of course nothing could have been more calculated to arouse my curiosity; a secret... about me... What could it be?

But Grandma forestalled questions by sending me to the bakery for fresh teacakes. We ate them liberally plastered with butter and strawberry jam, which successfully diverted my attention, so I forgot about the secret in the bible – at least for the time being. Anyway, I was too absorbed in various activities to dwell upon mysterious secrets.

The South Shore Baptist Church was the Gibson family's church; as well as services and prayer meetings, it provided members and Sunday school scholars with an active social life. During the week, I went to rehearsals at Sunday school for a Christmas concert. I had been given the leading role of the wizard in The Enchanted Pool which, Mother said, should suit me very well as I was very good at showing off. She was right. There was nothing that I liked better than creating an impression and gaining attention, especially at school.

Each week the girl with the most red, silver or gold stars to her credit gained the merit badge. My adoration for Miss Higham was my spur; I worked hard to win her smiling approval and my behaviour was impeccable, so, almost every Friday, I arrived home wearing the merit badge.

Mother was far from impressed. In her opinion, it was a pity that I didn't behave at home as well as I did at school. Again she was right. At home I was frequently awarded a dose of the strap for giving cheeky back answers to Mother.

The leather strap, used for sharpening Dad's shaving razor, had an additional duel role: as well as an instrument of punishment, it was used as a warning threat. It hung on a hook by the fireplace; if you started to misbehave, Mother took it from the hook and draped it over the fireguard to warm up for action. You ignored the warning at your peril and went to school with strap marks up your legs.

It never occurred to me that my home behaviour could be made known elsewhere, until Mother went to Revoe School and revealed my true character. The episode that triggered this seems ridiculous now, but discipline and rules were strict in those days, especially in our house. One of the rules was that, if someone gave you money, it must not be spent without permission. I broke the rule and got found out.

A kind neighbour for whom I often ran errands had given me three pence, which I spent on a visit to the Lido swimming pool. My crime was revealed when I arrived home with wet hair. Mother instantly demanded to know where I had got the money to go swimming. A tremendous row followed. Guilty and furious at my own wet-haired stupidity, I yelled that I could do what I liked with my money because I had earned it. But Mother had the last word. 'Right, lady.' She hung the strap on the fireguard. 'Your dad can deal with you. Get to bed!'

When Dad came in from the shop, I listened at the top of the stairs and heard Mother tell him that she was at her wit's end with my behaviour and that it was high time he gave me a good hiding. I grinned to myself and went back to bed. I knew how Dad would deal with me: I would get nothing more than a gentle reproach and a plea to be a good girl in future. And so it was.

No doubt Dad's failure to sort me out with the strap was why Mother went to Miss Dobson for help.

One day Miss Dobson appeared in our classroom and asked Miss Higham if she might borrow her monitor. As holder of the merit badge I was the monitor, so I stood to receive Miss Dobson's command. 'Oh, yes.' She turned to Miss Higham. 'I wanted to speak to you about that child.' I sat down again. I couldn't hear what Miss Dobson was saying to Miss Higham, but I was uncomfortably aware that something was wrong.

After Miss Dobson had gone, without giving me the monitor errand, I lifted my burning face from my book and stole a glance at Miss Higham; she was looking sadly at me. When the class made for the door at home time she kept me behind, so I knew that I was in trouble about something, but I couldn't think what it might be. I got a shock when Miss Higham told me, 'Your mother's been to see Miss Dobson. She said you are badly behaved and cheeky at home. I can hardly believe that of you. Won't you try to do better?'

I barely heard the rest of what she said; I was too appalled to take it in. The fact that Miss Higham now knew what I was really like and was disappointed in me was more than I could bear. I stood, head down in shamed silence, until she released me on my promise that I would not give any more cheek to Mother.

On the way home, I wept furious tears at what Mother had done. I did not see her visit to Miss Dobson as a cry for help; in my view, she had deliberately destroyed my adored teacher's good opinion of me, so I was going to pay her back with even worse behaviour.

During the following weeks, I got round my promise to Miss Higham by replacing verbal cheek with silent insolence, which infuriated Mother.

Then something totally unexpected happened. Mother made a dress for me to wear at the Sunday school's Christmas party. It was a beautiful dress made of green taffeta covered with a cloud of paler green net. There was ribbon trimming round the short sleeves and two broad bands of satin ribbon ran round the full skirt. I could hardly believe that such a wonderful dress was mine, especially as I knew perfectly well that I did not deserve it.

I puzzled over this until suddenly a thought struck me: I had never heard of an olive branch, but it came into my mind that the dress was meant to show that Mother wanted to be friends with me. The more I thought about it, the better I liked the idea; it gave me a warm feeling. I decided that, from now on, my behaviour was going to be faultless. I was going to obey cheerfully and do jobs like the washing up – which I detested – without being told. It was my way of showing Mother that I had caught her wavelength and was signalling back.

In the few days left before Christmas, I did all I could to help Mother. We didn't exchange a single cross word and she was pleased with my willing help. I had always felt that I was somehow on the edge of life in our house, as if I didn't quite belong there; but now that I was receiving approval, instead of being frowned upon, I felt included within family life. I enjoyed that, as well as the novelty of being good.

The Saturday before Christmas was the occasion of the year at our church. It began in the afternoon with a bazaar held in the schoolroom now a-sparkle with a Christmas tree and festive with looped garlands. Dozens of people crowded the stalls presided over by the ladies who had made the embroidered cushion covers, sideboard runners, tea cosies and tray cloths on sale. The ladies greatly admired my party dress as I preened my way round the stalls.

Down the middle of the room, trestle tables were set for

the party tea, with potted meat sandwiches, red and green jellies, and gorgeous cream cakes on three-tiered stands.

Teatime came at last. We stood behind our chairs and sang, 'Be present at our table, Lord,' then we sat down to eat. The chapel ladies came round with cups of tea; they made sure that we children ate sandwiches before they allowed us to dive into the jelly and cakes. I thought that the ladies looked very odd wearing flowered pinafores and last year's Sunday hats; but Dad said that none of the ladies would dream of appearing on sacred premises without a hat, whether it was for a divine service or a chapel tea.

After tea came the concert, in which I participated in all the songs and dances as well as playing my part as a wizard. The audience clapped appreciation of everything and Mrs Brammer, our producer, was presented with a box of chocolates. She organised all the Sunday school's social activities and we children enjoyed everything as much as she did.

After the concert, I swapped my wizard costume for my party dress and joined in the games. I had a wonderful time rushing hither and thither with the crisp green net of my flying skirts surprising my bare arms. And didn't I just enjoy the envious glances from girls in dull wool jumper suits at the green glory of my dress until, during a boisterous game, a surreptitious hand tore my dress – which served me right for showing off. Fortunately only the net part of my dress was torn and Mother later repaired it. The party ended with carol singing, then we went home with 'Merry Christmas!' ringing joyously in our ears.

Margaret and I always remembered it as the Christmas of the Singer dolls: we had seen them in the window when Mother was buying cotton reels at Singer's shop. How we had yearned after those beautifully dressed dolls with their golden curls and eyes that opened and shut. We had never dreamed that such expensive dolls could be ours, but to our amazed delight we found them beside our beds on Christmas morning.

It was only years later that we realised how Mother must have had to pinch and scrape to buy the dolls, because Dad's furniture business was suffering from Blackpool's seasonal loss of trade. No one wanted to buy unnecessary goods during the lean months spent struggling to survive until, with the visitors' return, money flowed back into the town.

On Christmas Day there was to be a party at Grandma's house. I could hardly wait to set off and, at last, we were all on our way with me skipping ahead clutching my nightie in a paper bag; I had been given permission to stay overnight at Grandma's, so my cup of joy was full and running over.

It was a gathering of the clan. There was a great deal of joyful reunion between Blackpool-based family and relatives who lived far away, such as Uncle Norman, who was a Baptist minister in a London church, and Uncle Jack, who had a chip shop in Spennymoor. Much to my delight, Uncle Lennie was there, twinkling and laughing in a Father Christmas hat.

There were several sittings for tea in the living room. Grandma carved a huge ham and urged everyone to eat up as there was plenty more. There were bowls of creamy trifle and a Christmas cake with a thick crown of snowy icing.

After tea we were to have a concert in the front room, where there was a piano. Uncle Lennie said that everyone had to take part; he was a member of a Black and White Minstrels concert party, so he knew how to organise a programme of entertainment with plenty of variety.

We all crammed into the front room. Uncle Lennie and my grown-up Cousin Jim set the ball rolling with a comedy song called 'The Hero and the Villain'. Uncle stuck a huge moustache on his face then, when Jim sang, 'I am the hero', Uncle joined in with a deep voice, 'and I am the villain bold!' as he twirled the ends of his moustache and wickedly rolled his eyes. The audience hissed the villain's dreadful doings and cheered the hero, who triumphed in the end. There were more songs, plus jokes and recitations. When it was my turn, I sang a hymn. Dad and I often sang hymns together, with him playing the piano. He could play by ear, so now he played while I sang:

> Jesus, tender shepherd, hear me,
> Bless thy little lamb tonight'

Out of the corner of my eye I could see Cousin Ted pretending to throw up over the back of a chair. 'OK, clever clogs,' I hissed beneath the applause for my contribution. 'I dare you to do a rude one.' He promptly leapt to his feet and declaimed:

> In nineteen thirty four, the soldiers went to war,
> They had no guns so they shot with their bums
> They didn't half feel sore.'

Then he was out of the room like lightning; his mother's hand just missed his backside as he whisked past. 'Eee! I wonder where our Ted got that?' Auntie Chrissie gave me a suspicious look, but this time I wasn't the culprit. A red-haired cousin, Margaret, had told Ted, George and me several rude rhymes whilst we were waiting for our turn at the tea table.

Later, when half-a-dozen of us were in bed in the attic, we heard all Margaret's rhymes again and committed them to memory.

Grandma puffed up to the attic with a generous supply of sweets and chocolate biscuits. She said that we could 'leave the gas on'. Electric lighting was still gas to Grandma. Then she clumped downstairs to the front room where the uncles were in full swing with 'The Cornish Floral Dance'.

We knew that we wouldn't get any more visitors from downstairs, so we climbed into bed for our feast and prepared to talk all night. I can't remember everything we talked about in our attic eyrie, but I recall every detail of Cousin Margaret's account of the operation she'd had for appendicitis. This included an enthralling description of something so horrifying it made our insides squirm: the nurse had put a rubber tube up her bottom and pumped in soapy water! We all gazed at Margaret with awe and a certain amount of envy; horrible though it all sounded, her experience was, at the same time, somehow mysterious and exciting. It set her apart from the rest of us.

Not to be outdone, Alan, my minister uncle's son, told us of his prowess at school; he was at a boarding school. We listened with respectful admiration as he described his heroic exploits and impressed upon us his popularity with the other boys. Alan was different from the rest of us; the only one of at least twenty cousins to enjoy the privilege of a public school education. Actually, he could not have enjoyed it at all: I later heard that he'd run away.

Still, each of us kept our own end up; I certainly contributed my share to the image-promoting whoppers we told each other that night. But none of us could cap Margaret's story, which was absolutely true.

When we at last settled down in our biscuit-crumby sheets, the drama of Margaret's operation was still going round in my head. I fell asleep hoping that one day I, too, might have an operation.

Chapter 4

After Christmas, I began to spend the evenings between tea and bedtime at my best friend's house, which meant that my sister was left on her own. I was absolutely amazed when Dad told me, 'Your mother's been weeping to me because Margaret has no one to play with.' Mother? Crying? I couldn't imagine her crying about anything; and I knew for certain that she would never have shown such concern for me.

I was used to Margaret getting all of Mother's attention, so I hadn't thought much about it, but what Dad had told me made me realise that, for Mother, there was a great difference between my sister and me. Anyway, I had to stay at home instead of going to my friend's house. I took my resentment out on Margaret, which got me into trouble with Mother and ended our truce.

The following spring we moved to a new modern semi in a residential road. It was only a few minute's walk from Dad's shop that he now rented separately from the upstairs rooms, which could be let as a flat.

We hadn't been in the new house for very long when I was taken out of school and sent to stay with Auntie Edna, Uncle Frank and Cousin Margaret at Brownhill, near Blackburn. I was not told the reason for this unexpected holiday, but I didn't wonder about it, I was so thrilled at the prospect of going to stay with Margaret. We were great friends. She often came to Grandma's with her parents and their black and white spaniel, Prince. I would wait outside Grandma's for their little car to appear with Prince's long floppy ears hanging out of the back window. As soon as the car stopped, Prince would leap out, give me an ecstatic tail-wagging greeting, and then hurtle into Grandma's house.

Prince loved being at Grandma's as much as I did. All the same, he knew to whom he really belonged. When Auntie, Uncle and Margaret went away on holiday, leaving him with Grandma, he would howl mournfully after the departing car. Then up to the attic he would go and wee on Grandma's bed, perhaps in protest at being left behind. Grandma smacked his nose and changed the bedclothes, while the smacked nose parked itself pathetically on every knee in the house seeking comfort. He got it: no one could resist those sad spaniel eyes and drooping ears.

He was a very naughty but lovable dog, and generous too; he never minded sharing his dog biscuits with Margaret and me.

Uncle Frank was a journalist on a Blackburn newspaper, so he and Auntie were well off compared with the Blackpool relatives. Their evenings were devoted to leisure and their lifestyle was a new experience for me.

After tea we all went across the road to the Baptist chapel, where Uncle and Auntie were members of the congregation.

There was always something going on: concerts, scout suppers, social evenings and there was a tennis court. Auntie and Uncle often played, with Margaret and me as ball girls. I tried to imagine my parents running and leaping on a tennis court, but I couldn't. Nor could I imagine them entertaining friends to supper as Uncle and Auntie did. They all seemed to have a lovely time; Margaret and I could hear them laughing when we were in bed. On those evenings, we never felt that we had been banished upstairs: we were given a most unusual treat.

Like a naughty conspirator, Auntie would whisper, 'How would you like to have a midnight feast in bed?' Then, from the supper table, we would be allowed to choose any cake we liked. We always chose gorgeous squishy cream puffs. We couldn't wait to get to bed and devour them; by the time midnight came, we had long been fast asleep.

There had been some talk of me joining Margaret at her school; the term still had some weeks to run. But Auntie said, 'Wouldn't you rather keep me company?' I didn't need persuading to do that. It was wonderful being with my vivacious, auburn-haired auntie. Like her brother, Lennie, she was always full of fun. Best of all was the loving attention that she gave to me. I was in clover.

Every morning I helped Auntie, then in the afternoons I went to The Glen. Prince led the way to the end of the road and across a patch of grass. Then we went down a steep path into a secret world, where a stream came wandering round a bend from a mysterious beyond, rippling and gliding over the stony bed. Trees leaned down the banks and a fallen tree, old and gnarled, rested across the sun-dappled dance of water.

No one came to disturb our blissful enjoyment of The Glen. Prince paddled up the stream, snuffling into holes in the bank, rooting under stones and snapping at flies. I gazed into small pools where tiny fishes flicked and strange insects skimmed the surface. There was the fallen tree trunk to be run across, or fallen off, and a flat rock beside the stream where I could sit and listen to the gurgling, chuckling water.

One day Auntie said, 'You'll miss The Glen when you go home.' I looked at her in dismay; was I about to be taken home? I didn't want to go home. But Auntie only gave me a hug and told Uncle that she'd never known such a bairn for going off on her own.

Uncle, too, was very kind. On Friday evenings he took us all to the cinema. We sat in the expensive seats and Uncle bought each of us a tube of Rolo chocolates. And all this when, at home, I should have been in bed! It was on one of those magical nights that I saw Ginger Rogers and Fred Astaire dancing in *Top Hat*. From then on, my ambition was to have dancing lessons and become a second Ginger Rogers.

One day, Auntie and I somehow got talking about families. She said, 'How would you like to have a little brother or sister?'

'We've got enough kids at our house,' I said emphatically. I was surprised by her query because it was obvious to me that being an adored only child, like Cousin Margaret, was far better than being one of a crowd.

A few days later, Auntie got a postcard. 'Guess what,' she beamed, 'you've got a baby brother!' I tried hard to look delighted because she seemed to think I should be; anyway, I didn't want to spoil her pleasure when she had been so loving and kind to me.

I was very sad when it was time for me to go home; Auntie, Uncle and Margaret were going on holiday. I paid a last visit to The Glen and sat beside the stream. 'We can't come again, I'm going home tomorrow,' I told Prince as he sat beside me. Sensing my sadness, he whined and licked comfort.

I loved The Glen so much that I wanted to take a bit of it home with me; I picked a leaf from a tree and put it in my knitted shoulder strap purse. Then I sadly said goodbye and went back to Auntie.

The following morning I was taken home. I got out of the car and went up the path. Just as I reached the front door, it opened. I stood appalled as Nurse Paget's grim face stared down at me; then she turned and marched upstairs.

I don't remember seeing the new baby, John. I was very

confused; nothing was as I had expected to find it. It seemed as if a great upheaval had taken place during my absence. The house was full of strangeness: Mother was in bed, awful Nurse Paget was back and a girl called Jenny was there (she lived in and did the housework).

Auntie, Uncle and Margaret had to go. As I watched them drive away, I wanted to howl after them like Prince did when he got left with Grandma. I wandered back into the house, but I didn't know where to put myself. My small bedroom was a no-go area: it was Nurse Paget's territory now. Nobody seemed to know where I was to sleep; there was no room for me in the back bedroom because Jenny and my sisters slept in there.

When Dad came home from the shop, he was as glad to see me as I was to see him.

After tea I proudly played a tune for him that Auntie had taught me on her piano.

'Hey! That's wonderful,' he exclaimed.

I was giving him an encore when Nurse Paget appeared and snapped, 'You've wakened Baby! And you are disturbing my patient.'

'Sorry, Nurse,' Dad said humbly. 'We didn't think.'

'Then please do so in future.'

She swept away and Dad said, 'Phew!' I sensed that he wasn't all that keen on Nurse Paget. We went upstairs and Dad made up a bed for me in the bathroom. He put two boards across the bath and padded them with blankets. Normally I would have enjoyed the novelty of sleeping in the bathroom, but that night it only added to the strangeness of everything. I lay on my wood board-bed, gazing at the white-tiled walls. Although I was glad to be with my dad, I missed Auntie. I yearned to be back in the happy world of Brownhill, to be with Prince in The Glen.

Suddenly I remembered my leaf. I slid off my bed, found my purse in my unpacked case and took out the leaf. Then I held it to my nose, closed my eyes, inhaled its leafy scent and imagined myself back in The Glen. Comfort – warm and peaceful – flowed into me. I got back into bed and drifted off to sleep.

I kept the leaf between the pages of a book, where it became a dried transparent wisp of its former self, but still a treasured link with my beloved Glen.

Fortunately Margaret and I didn't have to suffer Nurse Paget for long; she left, and so did Jenny.

I suppose that paying a resident nurse, a doctor's bill and a home help, as well as two rents, proved too much for my parents' financial resources; which was probably why we moved back to the shop, where the flat above was still unoccupied.

Autumn came. With the departure of the visitors, people had no money to spare for furniture when food, rent etc. were the priorities, so Dad's shop lost trade.

In an attempt to drum up business, he had some advertisements, called handbills, printed and offered me a ha'penny a hundred to deliver them round the neighbourhood.

I set off round the streets, popping a handbill into each letterbox. One house was empty with a 'To Let' sign. There didn't seem to be much point in leaving a handbill at an empty house, so I walked past; then I changed my mind, turned back and dropped one in.

Before long I discovered that Dad was in debt. One Saturday morning he brought the post from behind the shop door into the living room. I was clearing the breakfast table, so I heard what came next.

'What is it?' Mother eyed the letter in Dad's hand.

'It's from Simpsons, a final demand.'(I knew that Simpsons supplied the furniture for Dad's shop.) He sank down on a chair, leaned his elbows on the table and put his

49

head in his hands. 'I can't pay. I don't know what I'm going to do.'

I knew that this was very serious indeed, because money problems were never discussed in front of us children. But now they were so worried that they hadn't even noticed that I was listening.

I washed up in the kitchen and wished that I could help Dad to pay his debt. I tried hard to think of a way to get some money. If only, I thought, I owned something valuable I could sell. Then suddenly I remembered my silver moon brooch! Grandma had given it to me for my birthday and it was my most precious possession. It had a little crescent moon mounted on a slim bar. I knew that it must be valuable because it was made of silver.

I went upstairs and took out my brooch. For a moment I wondered how I could bear to part with it; then I thought of how relieved and grateful Dad would be when I gave him the money to pay his debt. I put the brooch in my pocket and set off for the shops in the town centre. I ignored cheap jewellery shops and made for a chandelier-lit emporium. I hovered apprehensively outside, then I took a deep breath and went in.

I stood daunted by the sparkling displays of rings, bracelets and necklaces. Then a voice said, 'May I help you?' A tall man was bending towards me over a glass-topped counter.

'Please, do you buy jewellery?' I managed to say.

'Sometimes. What do you wish to sell?' The amusement in his pale blue eyes almost undermined my shaky courage, but I dragged out my brooch and put it on the counter. He looked down at it. 'Got it out of a lucky bag, did you?'

'No!' I felt my cheeks flame. 'My grandma gave it to me; it's real silver.'

'Silver!' He laughed. 'Cheap junk. No good to me.'

I grabbed my brooch and fled, crying tears of humiliation and disappointment. I had so firmly imagined selling my brooch and running home in triumph to rescue Dad from debt and worry; the possibility of it not happening had never occurred to me. I wandered miserably round the town and then I went home.

Dad met me at the shop door and pulled me in. His face was a-shine with joy and relief. He could hardly get the words out as he told me, 'I was so desperate, I prayed for help. The minute I'd finished praying, a customer came in and spent eighty pounds!'(The average weekly wage was about £2, so a cash sale of this magnitude was a miracle for Dad.) 'This means I can settle my debt. Oh! The power of prayer,' he exulted.

Perhaps it was more a case of God helping those who help themselves, because one of the handbills had brought the customer. A wealthy lady who'd come from abroad had taken the empty house that I had almost missed out when I was delivering the handbills. When I told Dad how I had changed my mind and left a handbill, he insisted that I had been the instrument of the Lord. He was convinced that 'divine intervention' had rescued him from debt. I didn't tell him about my humiliating attempt to sell my brooch.

Of course I was very glad indeed for Dad, but I couldn't help feeling jealous of God. I'd done my best, but He had done it all and now He was getting all the credit and gratitude that could have been mine had I saved the family fortunes. But really it was all for the best; Dad was out of debt and I still had my moon brooch. Although I now knew that it wasn't silver, I didn't care; Grandma had given it to me and that was its real value.

Another gift from Grandma, the following Christmas, was a pretty pink satin handkerchief pouch. Mother was highly indignant because Grandma hadn't given presents to my sisters and brother. Dad was told that he must stop

Grandma giving presents to me in future; he pointed out that she had too many grandchildren to buy for all.

'She can always find the money to buy for her,' Mother jerked a thumb at me, 'and for that lot at Lytham Road. She gave your Chrissie a china tea set; ridiculous extravagance! And they're all as bad, buying each other presents they can't afford. Then what happens?' She turned to me. 'They can't pay the rent, so they have to go borrowing from your Uncle Lennie.'

I knew that Mother was trying to lower Grandma and my aunties in my eyes when she got going with her contemptuous criticisms, but she didn't succeed. I didn't care if they were 'daft with money'. Nor did I think my cousins were 'neglected' because they slept 'in a mucky cellar' – a privilege that I envied and shared whenever Grandma's attic was full of visitors' children.

I resented Mother's scornful criticisms of Grandma and my aunties; they loved me and I loved them. I knew that I belonged with them in their happy world, just as I knew that I did not belong at home where the atmosphere was cold and joyless.

Even Dad seemed distanced from me now; most evenings he was out at prayer meetings or other church affairs. My sense of not belonging grew and I began to wonder who I really was. *Perhaps*, I thought, *I am an orphan or a lost child, and one day I will be found by my real parents*.

It was now that I remembered the secret in Grandma's bible. The more I thought about it, the more certain I became that the secret would tell me who I really was. I decided that the first chance I got, I would sneak a look into that bible. But it was easier said than done; Grandma was always around when I was at her house.

Anyway, Mother had curtailed my visits to Lytham Road; she said that I should spend less time there and more at home so that I could help to pack up ready for moving house.

Mother didn't like living at the shop, or anywhere else, for long. Her complaint, 'I'm fed up with living in this hole,' was always to signal a move in future years.

So we moved into a small modern house round the corner from the shop, which Dad again rented separately from the upstairs flat. However, before Mother had time to get fed up with the new house, we scuttled back to the shop. Dad's rescue from debt did not alter the fact that trade was poor, so payment of two rents could not be afforded.

But, just before we moved back to the shop, something unexpected happened.

Chapter 5

One day, when I got home from school, there was no one in. Packing for the move had begun; there were half-filled cartons on the living room floor and papers from Dad's desk were piled on the table. A large envelope had slid off the pile to the floor. I picked it up.

I'm not sure now what went through my mind when I saw 'Certificates' written on the envelope, but something impelled me to look inside it. Perhaps I was seeking a clue to the secret in Grandma's bible, or maybe I was just being nosy. I can't remember. Anyway, the envelope was unsealed so, although I knew that I should not be snooping, I fished inside it.

There were several birth certificates including mine, which gave only my name plus date and place of birth. (This was the basic 'sixpenny certificate': those giving information about parents cost more.) Then I found one headed 'Entry of Death.' I was surprised to discover that death, as well as birth, needed a certificate; I examined it curiously to see who had died.

It was a lady called Emily Gibson. The date of her death caught my eye: it was ten days after the day on which I had been born. I couldn't understand the strange words in the 'Cause of Death' section, but in another I read that Emily had been the wife of Edward Gibson. My dad! I stared in amazement. How could that be? I read it all again, then it dawned on me: if the Emily who died soon after I was born had been married to my dad, then she must have been my mother!

I distinctly remember that, although it was a shock, far greater was the relief that came with the realisation that the woman I called 'Mother' was not my mother. I was not her child and now I knew why she didn't like me: it was because she was my stepmother. Stepmothers in the stories I'd read were always unkind or even cruel to their stepchildren.

I stood with my thoughts in a whirl until I heard the back door open. Hastily I thrust the certificates back in the envelope and dropped it on the table just as Mother came in. She eyed me suspiciously. 'What are you doing?' I stared dumbly at her: I was seeing her with new eyes. She told me to stop gawping at her and go to the shop, where Dad wanted me to deliver a hearthrug to a customer.

When I arrived at the shop, I didn't tell Dad about my discovery. I had no doubt that I had found out the secret in Grandma's bible – the secret I wasn't supposed to know – and if I let on that I knew, I would have to admit that I had been snooping. I felt very guilty about it all, so I kept quiet.

Yet I badly wanted to know about my real mother. Who was she, what was she like, what had happened to her? But I wasn't supposed to know that she had existed, so I couldn't ask. The secrecy and silence surrounding her seemed to deny that she had ever been there at all. I kept my eyes and ears open for clues that might tell me something about her. Then, a few days after we returned to the shop, it happened...

Instead of doing the teatime washing up, I had sneaked off to the library to change my book. When I got back, Mother banished me to bed, which was exactly what I had planned would happen. I often got myself sent to bed so that I could read in peace.

I knew that Dad would get a report on my conduct so, when he came in from a church meeting, I listened at the top of the stairs as Mother listed my sins and told him,

'She's always got her nose stuck in a book.'

Dad said mildly, 'Her mother was very fond of reading.' That was all he said, but hearing my mother actually spoken of brought her out of nowhere; she had really been there! And she had liked reading. Well, so did I; it was a link between us. More than a link; it was a bond that somehow gave me a sense of belonging to my Emily mother.

I wish now that I had admitted my discovery of the secret, then all would have been brought into the open and I would not have had to wait for so long to learn more about my mother; nor would I have had to carry the guilt of knowing what I was not supposed to know. For the following five years, I kept it all in my head and never once let it out, though of course it did not entirely absorb my thoughts; I was very young, so a child's interests and activities were to the fore.

Mother's complaint to Dad about my perpetual reading resulted in his confiscation of my library ticket. He said, 'You can have it back when you show yourself more willing to help Mother.' Then he ordered delivery of *Arthur Mee's Children's Newspaper*, which, he said, contained more worthwhile reading matter than the books I got from the library. No doubt it did, but I did not appreciate its worthiness, nor did Margaret.

However, we soon found reading matter to our taste on the glass-panelled shelves of the bookcase in our living room. There was a variety of choice, especially if you liked Victorian religious publications, and we certainly did.

There were penny paperbacks for children such as *Christie's Organ* and *Jessica's First Prayer*. In these and other gripping stories, children suffered dire poverty, emotional deprivation and fatal illness. There were heartrending deathbed scenes in which children died beautifully, forgiving everybody, before being borne aloft by angels to pearly gates opening wide to receive them. We wept over the deaths, enjoyed the drama and ignored the religious bits encouraging us to be good and merit those children's heavenly reward – a prospect that did not enthral us.

Another favourite was our 'awful history book'. We called it that because the bits that interested us all began with, 'The awful history of H' (or another initial). It was actually a Temperance publication full of moral warning against the abuse of alcohol. The awful histories were printed in italics, so it was easy to miss out the religious stuff in ordinary print and concentrate on the italicised horrors, which we did with immense enjoyment.

We absorbed with relish the terrible degradation into which the families of alcoholics sank. There were homes where orange boxes were the only furniture, a heap of rags on the floorboards the only bed, and starving families wept in despair beside fireless grates. We had no idea that such things really happened, or that our own grandma's earlier history was similar to those we were reading.

In *The Sunday Book* (which must have provided permitted fiction entertainment for churchgoing Victorians) we had our first encounter with Napoleon, in a dramatic story about a girls' school in France. It began with a punishment parade worthy of our Miss Dobson. Before the assembled school, one of the girls, found guilty of some misdemeanour, was ceremoniously stripped of her 'violet sash of honour', which was then trampled into the dust of the yard. Enter Napoleon, who cleared her name – I don't remember how – and restored the sash to great acclaim. Heady stuff! Well, it was to us; we often enacted the sash-stripping scene using a mauve ribbon off a chocolate box.

It wasn't long before Dad cancelled the unread worthy newspaper and gave me back my library ticket which, with the approach of spring, was not in daily use because I was going to Mrs Brammer's rehearsals for a May Day celebration to be held in our Sunday school. It promised to be very special compared to the usual May Day affairs, when girls formed small groups and took to the streets with maypoles. The girl chosen to be the May Queen dressed up in an old net curtain and sat on a stool, holding the maypole, whilst the rest danced round her and sang, 'Dancing round the maypole merrily we go…' The maypole was usually an upended yard brush with a few wild flowers stuck in the bristles; ribbons were lengths of string or coloured wool.

But Mrs Brammer's maypole was the real thing. It stood tall in its solid base, topped with hoops entwined with flowers from which hung red and blue satin ribbons, one for each dancer. Margaret and I were dancers, but for us those ribbons were a problem: they had to be paid for – four pence each.

We knew that our parents couldn't afford eight pence just for ribbons. We didn't even think of asking; how could we when we were down to potatoes with Bisto gravy for dinner and mustard on bread for tea?

Rehearsals went ahead and everyone, except us, had paid for their ribbons. Eight pence, and how on earth I was going to find it, was all that I could think of; it haunted me night and day.

Then suddenly my problem was solved. One evening, after school, I carried a fireside fender set to one of Dad's customers. As well as the fender there were two box seats, one for each end of the fender. I couldn't carry them all at once, so I made three deliveries. The customer, a handsome young man, gave me a shilling! I should have thought myself well rewarded with a penny.

How grateful I was to that generous young man; and what a relief it was to be able to give Mrs Brammer the eight pence. Twelve pence made a shilling, so I had four pence change, which I hid behind a loose brick in the washhouse – in case there should be a future unexpected need.

Shortage of money was an ongoing problem, so, when the school's summer break came, I went looking for Lobby Lud. A photograph of him, wearing a trilby hat tipped over one eye, appeared daily in the *News Chronicle* delivered to our house. Lists of times and places where Lobby could be spotted were provided. You had to carry a copy of the paper; if you found him, you had to say, 'You are Mister Lobby Lud and I claim the *News Chronicle* prize.' I'm not sure how much it was – it could have been five or ten pounds; anyway, it was a fortune in my eyes.

I spent many hours roaming around Blackpool looking for Lobby. I never found him; but somebody else who was hunting around the streets found me.

One day, on my way home from a fruitless search for Lobby, I stopped as I always did to tipple-tail over a round iron bar set between concrete posts outside a builder's yard near to our shop. Over and over I whirled. When I stopped, a tall young man was standing watching me and smiling. He said, 'My! You are very good at that.' I gave him a few more whirls, partly as a reward for his admiration and partly because I enjoyed showing off. When I stopped, he was still watching and smiling. He looked very smart in his brown suit and trilby hat and he had a friendly sort of face. He said, 'If you come with me, I'll give you a penny.'

I thought that he wanted me to run an errand or do a job of some sort. I was always glad of the opportunity to earn a penny, so I willingly went with the friendly smiling man. He took my hand and we went along the road. My dad could easily have seen us had we walked past the shop, but we turned off the main road and went along the back street behind the houses and shops. It was familiar territory; my friends and I often played there in a secluded recess that ran from the back street to a garage. We liked the recess because there was no one there to shout at us to go away when we played noisy games.

The man took me into the recess; we stopped a few feet away from the garage. 'Wait there a moment,' he said. Then he went to the garage and pulled at the double doors. He tugged several times, but the doors wouldn't open. He stood with his back to me for a moment or two, and then he turned to face me.

Shocked and horrified, I froze in terror. There was an awful red thing with a snout sticking out of his unfastened trousers. Still smiling, he moved towards me. Somehow I dragged my feet off the ground and ran.

Back to the main road I flew and into our shop. Sobbing and shaking, I flung myself at Dad. 'What is it?' he asked, his arms went around me.

'A man—' I gasped.

Dad had me out of the door in a flash. 'Show me where.' We ran to the garage but the man had gone. 'Did he touch you?' Dad asked grimly. Words seemed to be stuck in my throat; I shook my head.

When we got back to the main road a policeman was coming towards us. Dad stopped him and said something I couldn't hear; but I heard the policeman tell Dad to take me to the police station. I was petrified.

Mother had often threatened me with, 'If you don't mend your ways, I'll fetch a policeman to you, then you'll be sent to a reformatory.' I thought that a reformatory was a prison where policemen took bad girls, so I was terrified of policemen, in case they found out that I was a bad girl and took me to a reformatory. If I had not still been in shock, I would have known that my dad would never have let anything of the sort happen to me; but Mother's threat was all that I could think of, so, by the time we arrived at the police station, I was numb with fear.

We were shown into an office. A stout policeman was sitting at a desk; he looked strange, not really like a policeman because he wasn't wearing a helmet. He was smiling.

He said, 'Come and sit beside me, luv. It's all right; nothing's going to happen to you. I'm just going to ask you a few questions, then you can go home with your dad.'

Perhaps there were no women officers in those days, but no woman could have been more kind and understanding than that policeman. He must have seen how frightened I was, so he straight away made me feel safe.

Dad sat next to me as the policeman gently questioned me. I described the man and what had happened right up to the point where he turned to face me by the garage.

But 'What did he do then?' floored me. I had no words to describe what I had seen; I had never seen anything like it. There was an uncomfortable silence, broken by an uneasy cough from Dad. Then the policeman said, 'Did he unfasten his trousers?' I nodded.

Thankfully there were no more questions. I just had to look at a book of photographs of men and say whether any of them looked like the man who'd frightened me. None of them did, but I wanted to help the friendly policeman, so I picked out a man wearing a trilby hat like the one worn by the man who smiled.

When the policeman saw us out, he said to Dad, 'You will warn your daughter, won't you, Sir? I don't need to tell you what might have happened.'

On the way home Dad said, 'I should have warned you before; you must never, never go anywhere with a stranger.' I had no idea of what might have happened to me, but I sensed that it was something terrible. Anyway, I had learned my lesson; in future I would never so much as speak to a stranger.

When we got home, Mother was in. She said, 'Where have you been all this time?' Then she looked at my face. I don't know what she saw there, but she immediately demanded, 'What's she been up to?'

Dad briefly told her about my encounter with the man and our visit to the police station. Just then the shop bell rang. When Dad had gone, Mother turned on me in fury. 'It would happen to you! It was your own fault. You should have had more sense.'

I was stunned. My own fault! Neither Dad nor the policeman had blamed me for what had happened. But the scornful disgust in Mother's eyes was undeniable.

It was my own fault. I burst into tears and ran out the back door. Straight to my grandma I ran. 'Why, bairn, what's the matter?' She held me as I wept. 'Tell me what's wrong.' Too much was whirling in my head. I couldn't tell her about the man, or the awful things that Mother had said. But Grandma comforted me. 'Never mind, pet. I'm here; I'm always here.'

For a long time afterwards, I was afraid to go to sleep. I kept dreaming that the man who smiled was standing at the end of my bed... smiling. And I never again played by the back street garage.

Chapter 6

Shortly before the Christmas of 1936 a royal scandal broke. Even children who didn't read the newspapers or listen to the news on the wireless knew what all the fuss was about. Our king, Edward, wanted to marry a twice-divorced American called Mrs Simpson and make her his queen.

In the ensuing furore, the nation took sides. At Revoe we supported those who were against the marriage. We were definitely anti-Mrs Simpson, because divorce was shocking; it was something that respectable people never did (it was almost unheard of in those days). As Christmas approached we carolled:

> Hark the herald angels sing,
> Mrs Simpson's pinched our king.

Indeed she had. Edward abdicated to marry her and his brother, George Duke of York, ascended the throne. His wife, Elizabeth, was no Mrs Simpson: she was the aristocratic daughter of an Earl, and her reputation was unblemished.

Coronation Day, 12 May 1937, just had to be fine, and it was. The sun, determined to be in on all the fun, got up early and shone on the festive scene. Patriotic red, white and blue was everywhere; flags waved, banners hung from windows and bunting criss-crossed streets.

A grand celebration was held on the Bloomfield Road football ground; hundreds of people were there. I sat with the massed children's choirs, high up in the spectator stands from where we had a splendid view of the folk dancing, gymnastic displays and a fancy dress parade. The events were interspersed with patriotic songs, which we choir members had been rehearsing for weeks, such as 'Rule Britannia'. One song proclaimed the loyalty of our far-flung colonies:

> From lands far away
> They are calling today
> Three cheers for the red, white and blue.

Best of all was the finale. A brass band struck up and columns of children wearing red, white or blue patches on their backs marched onto the ground and formed a rectangle in the centre. Then the music stopped. Drums rolled, softly at first, then they rose to a thundering crescendo. CLASH went the cymbals. Instantly the children crouched on all fours and there, before our eyes, was a gigantic Union Jack with every red and blue stripe perfectly outlined against a white background; there wasn't a wiggle anywhere. Everyone cheered and clapped like mad; then we all sang 'God Save the King', with the band booming every note fit to rock the Tower.

Afterwards, children went to their schools for a Coronation Tea. At Revoe our goodies were presented in white cake boxes, previously decorated by ourselves with potato cutouts dipped in red and blue paint. We all received a coronation mug with a picture of the King and Queen on it.

The following week, Margaret and I went to a cinema to see the newsreel pictures of the Coronation. We saw the King and Queen in their crowns and robes, standing on the balcony outside Buckingham Palace. Their daughters, princesses Elizabeth and Margaret, were there too, wearing coronets and miniature robes.

My sister and I had always been fascinated by the princesses; our names and ages were the same, so we felt an affinity with them. We treasured all our glossy birthday cards depicting the princesses charmingly posed in dresses with layers of frills. In our younger days those 'frill frocks', as we called them, had been the subject of a great deal of squabbling because, when we played our favourite game of pretending to be the princesses, I, as the elder (and bossier) princess, had always insisted that my frock had more frills than Margaret's. We were now too old for that, but we still adored the princesses, so, when a royal visit to Blackpool was announced, we were filled with the excited anticipation of actually seeing them.

The great day came. All the town's schoolchildren were lined up on the royal route, the Promenade. I stood with Margaret; we waited for what seemed like hours as we clutched the small flags we'd been given. Miss Dobson had told us that as soon as the royal car appeared we must wave our flags and cheer.

We craned our necks along the empty Promenade for a first sight. Then suddenly there was the open-topped car coming towards us... it was in front of us... rolling past. Margaret and I did not wave our flags or cheer; we stood stunned with disbelief: the princesses were not there. Furthermore, we had expected to see the King and Queen wearing their jewelled crowns and ermine robes; instead we saw just an ordinary couple. The King wore a dark suit; he was hatless and his hair looked as if it had been cut too short. He seemed small, insignificant, not a bit like a king. The Queen wore a blue dress and a feathery hat; she smiled at us and raised her hand in a slow half-wave, but the King stared ahead and up at the Tower. There wasn't much flag-waving or cheering, so probably other children, too, felt let down by royal failure to fulfil expectation.

By the time summer came, Grandma wasn't well. Although Vera was back to help, she wasn't much use; she wandered about taking ages to clear tables and wash up. So, when the August school holiday came, Dad said that I could stay with Grandma and help her.

Mother was not pleased at losing my help; she did not like housework, so, during school holidays, endless cleaning up was added to my normal tasks. But Dad said that Grandma's need was greater than Mother's, so off I went.

Each morning, when the alarm clock awoke Grandma and me in the attic, she was struggling to get out of bed so I told her, 'Take your time, Grandma.' Then I ran downstairs, helped Vera with the visitors' breakfasts and worked with a will all day.

Uncle Lennie arrived and Grandma insisted that I went with him and my cousins on outings to the Ice Drome show, to Pablo's and on picnics, so, as always, I revelled in life at Lytham Road, especially with Uncle there to complete my happiness.

He had a serious talk with Grandma; he said that it was time for her to give up the boarding house. So, when the season ended, she moved to a gloomy upstairs flat on Lytham Rd.

On Saturday afternoons, I went to the flat and sat with Grandma. She was too tired now to make quilts, but we had our usual Saturday feast of strawberry jam and teacakes; then we sat quietly, with Grandma dozing by the fire and me sitting by the window. Opposite was a cobbler's shop; in the window a small gnome sat tapping with a hammer on a tiny shoe. I was fascinated by that merry-faced little man and his mechanical tapping; he held me in thrall until twilight came, Grandma woke up and it was time for me to go home.

One Saturday evening Grandma fastened the buttons on my coat, gave me a hug and said, 'Now, pet, I want you to do something for me: I want you to be a good girl.'

I knew at once what had happened. Mother had carried out her threat to give Grandma my 'true character'. She had been holding this over my head for some time, and not without reason. Since my discovery that she was my stepmother, my behaviour had worsened. The traditional image of the cruel stepmother I'd got from stories had certainly fuelled my dislike of mine and increased my insolence. I had defiantly told myself that she was not my mother so she couldn't tell me what to do. Of course, I had to do as I was told or she gave me a good thumping.

But thumping was nothing compared to telling Grandma how awful I was, so now I stood burning with shame and fury as Grandma pleaded, 'Oh, bairn, you must be good; you will try, won't you pet?' Then she let me go and I ran crying from the flat.

The following Saturday, for the first time ever, I didn't want to go to Grandma; I was too ashamed to face her, but I had no choice. Dad, assuming that I was going as usual, gave me a small white package with a chemist's label on it and said, 'Your grandma's poorly, so she has to take this medicine.'

I put it in my coat pocket and reluctantly set off. Then I had an idea: I would get George and Ted to go with me. I reasoned that, with my cousins there, Grandma would not go on at me with more shaming pleas for me to be good.

I collected George and Ted, but we didn't go to Grandma, we went to the Plaza cinema; the boys didn't want to miss an episode of a *Flash Gordon* serial. I didn't need persuading to go with them. I told myself that I would pop Grandma's medicine in on my way home. But when we came out of the cinema, leaving Flash Gordon in terrible danger from Martian monsters, the prospect of seeing next week's episode completely filled my head, so I forgot about Grandma's medicine.

When I got home, Dad asked how Grandma was. Then I remembered. I let out a gasp of dismay; my hand flew to my coat pocket. 'Oh! I forgot—'

'Of course you think too much of your grandma to forget her medicine when she's ill,' Mother said sarcastically.

Never had I run so fast to Grandma. I was out of breath when I reached the flat and hurtled up the stairs into the living room. Grandma was not there!

Auntie Chrissie appeared from the kitchen. She said, 'Your grandma's in bed, pet. She's poorly and very tired, so don't stop long.' I had expected to find Grandma sitting by the fire as usual; Dad hadn't said that she was ill enough to be in bed.

I gave the medicine to Auntie and went into the bedroom. It was small and dimly lit by an unshaded light bulb hanging from the ceiling. Grandma was lying in a tumbled bed that took up nearly all the space. As I went in, she struggled up and heaved over a chamber pot beside the bed, then she sank back exhausted. She tried to lift her arms towards me. 'My bairn,' she said faintly.

I stood shocked and frightened by the sight of Grandma's suffering. Suddenly I desperately wanted to put everything back the way it was, with Grandma sitting beside the fire in her black dress and buttoned shoes. 'Please get up, Grandma,' I pleaded frantically. 'Come and sit by the fire.'

'Is it time for chapel? Find my shoes, there's a good girl.' She tried to sit up. Auntie came in and told me that Grandma was to be taken to *her* house, where she could be looked after by all her family. I was very relieved. Grandma would be out of this awful room and back where she belonged, so she would soon get better. I kissed her soft wrinkled cheek and went home.

One morning, a few days later, I came downstairs and began to get ready for school. Dad was standing by the window, gazing out at the frosty garden. I stood in front of the wall mirror and started brushing my hair.

'Your grandma went to Heaven early this morning,' Dad said quietly.

I stopped brushing and stared at my face in the mirror. I barely took in something Dad was saying about Grandma being released from suffering.

Just then Mother came downstairs. Dad always gave her tea before she got up; she put her cup and saucer on the table and told him, 'That tea was much too weak; you didn't put enough in the pot.' Then she turned to me. 'You'd better get a move on or you'll be late for school.' As if nothing had happened; as if my world hadn't suddenly fallen apart!

I choked back the howl I could feel rising in my throat and made for the toilet off the kitchen. Inside I locked the door. Drops of condensation from the kettle in the kitchen were sliding down the shiny orange and white-papered walls. I stared hard at the drops, widening my eyes in a desperate attempt to hold back the tears burning to spring forth. But the tears sliding down the wall released mine and I wept in an agony of grief for my grandma.

When the worst was over, I mopped my eyes and flushed the toilet so that Mother would think that I had been paying a normal visit. For some reason I didn't want her to know that I had been crying for my grandma.

I cried all the way to school. When I arrived, the playground was empty so I was late, but I was past caring as I trailed up the stairs to the hall where assembly was almost over.

I was not the only latecomer. On the platform, Miss Dobson was thundering at a trembling first-form girl. A teacher pushed me forward. 'Here's another one, Miss Dobson.' She dismissed the other girl with ten black stars and turned to me.

'Slug-a-bed!' she bellowed as I stood sobbing before her. 'You are a disgrace to the school!' I was too devastated by my loss to care what she called me, or to offer an explanation for my lateness. Anyway, Miss Dobson never asked for explanations; I was late and there was no excuse for that, so it was ten black stars for me. If it had been a thousand I would not have cared; nothing could have made that day any blacker for me.

Black seemed to be everywhere; all the relations who came for Grandma's funeral wore black. Children did not go to funerals, but Dad took me to church the following Sunday when a memorial service was held for Grandma. There was a black cover on the pulpit's bible desk. The minister said, 'Mrs Gibson has passed to her reward and rest; we shall now sing for her the hymn *In heavenly love abiding*. He also said that Christ would comfort us and wipe away our tears.

I didn't want Grandma abiding in Heaven, I wanted her here with me, so I was not comforted. Every night in bed, I cried myself to sleep.

One evening, Auntie Chrissie came with a basket, in which was Dad's share of Grandma's few possessions. Amongst them was the alarm clock that had awakened Grandma and me in the attic on so many summer mornings. Dad gave the clock to me.

Nothing could have been less cuddly than that cold, hard bell-topped clock; but every night I hugged it close. Instead of crying myself to sleep, I gazed at the friendly green glow of the luminous dial in the darkness beneath my bedclothes. It seemed to bring Grandma near to me and I fell asleep comforted.

All the same, I felt sad and empty, so what happened next could have been an attempt to cheer me up with a bit of special attention. It could have been Mother's idea, but it was probably Dad's. One Saturday afternoon Mother took me – just me – to the cinema to see *The Prince and the Pauper* starring Errol Flynn.

I knew that I did not belong, as my siblings did, so I did not expect special attention from Mother, nor had she ever taken me anywhere, so I was very surprised. Furthermore, Mother went out of her way to be friendly to me. I was delighted.

Sadly she was rewarded by having her purse stolen from her pocket, probably when we were leaving the cinema amongst a crowd. But she didn't spoil the occasion by dwelling on what must have been a loss that she could ill afford. On that day I felt close to Mother and I wished we could always be on friendly terms. It didn't happen again, but I never forgot that unusual outing.

Chapter 7

Although I missed Grandma very much indeed, I still had everyone at Lytham Road. In addition, I had another auntie to whom I turned for consolation. Auntie Jessie (the one married to the ex-footballer) was a kind, motherly soul who lived a couple of streets away from us. I often went to her house and she always found time to talk to me. She was also the only sister-in-law with whom Mother had a good relationship; they got on well together and Mother depended on Auntie for friendship and support.

I remember that when Dad was taken dreadfully ill with food poisoning, Mother cried in terror to me, 'Go and fetch Auntie Jessie!' She came at once and took charge, as she did when Mother decided to move out of the shop again and chose the wrong time to do it.

A house next door but one to our shop was to let. It was on a block of superior Edwardian houses, so of course Mother couldn't wait to move in; despite the fact that Dad was not in a fit state to cope with what was practically a DIY removal. He had got a hernia from lifting heavy furniture in the shop, so he was waiting to go into hospital for an operation. Nevertheless, a date was fixed for the move and a man was hired to help Dad with the piano and other heavy furniture.

Unfortunately, the hospital sent for Dad to go in on the afternoon of removal day, but it still went ahead. He spent the morning heaving furniture and went to the hospital in the afternoon. Mother looked after the shop and Auntie

Me with Grandma shortly after my mother died.

A heavy handful for my valiant grandma who looked after me until I was eighteen months old.

Dad with his second wife and their daughter, Margaret, on his knee. My stepmother holding me – something she never did so I was very surprised.

Me in the year I started going to school.

With my half-sister Margaret, who got bossed around by me when her mother wasn't there.

Me and Margaret with Uncle Lennie.

Blackpool boarding house cousins. My buddies George and Ted, left and right. Me next to George with Prince at my feet.

Grandma with naughty Prince who got his nose smacked.

Jessie came to help with meals and to look after John, who was still too young to go to school.

Children were not allowed on adult wards, so I couldn't go with Mother to visit Dad.

After he'd had his operation, I anxiously checked the hospital list published in the evening paper. Few people had telephones in those days, so the list provided patients' progress under headings such as, 'Poorly', 'As well as can be expected', 'Doing well' and 'Discharged'. Thankfully Dad's name was never on the first list and he was soon doing well. When he came home, he had to spend a few days in bed. Auntie went home at teatime to feed her own family, so, when I got back from school, I made our tea and looked after Dad until Mother came in from the shop.

I was so glad to have my dad back that I couldn't do enough for him. I sped up and down stairs with cups of tea and snacks and remade his rumpled bed. He was impressed and grateful for my attention. He told me, 'At this rate, when you grow up, you could have a really beautiful character.'

Me with a beautiful character? I was amazed! But I liked the idea, so straight away I decided that, from now on, my behaviour was going to be perfect and my life was going to be devoted to helping others.

Downstairs, I started work on the new self-sacrificing me by doing some cleaning for Mother. Whilst I worked, I sang a hymn: 'Take my hands and let them move at the impulse of Thy love.' I sang at the top of my voice so that Dad would hear and know that I was working on the development of my beautiful character.

I knew that, if I was going to do it properly, I must stop cheeking Mother and cheerfully do all I could to help her without being told. That was a tall order for me, but I was determined to do my best. Anyway, I really did want to make things better between Mother and me, as they had been on the day she'd taken me to the cinema.

I decided to start my new approach to Mother by doing something special for her, to show that I wanted us to be friends. Perhaps, I thought, I could surprise her with a present, but what to give her was a problem. Then I had an idea: child-like, I decided to give her something that I would have loved to have for myself.

It was a cake – a cream meringue. I had often wished to have one when I had gazed longingly at the snow-white shells clasping creamy curls in the cake shop's window. But they were expensive, three pence each, so meringues had never appeared on our table.

As it happened, I had the money to buy one for Mother: behind the loose brick in the washhouse, I still had the four pence I'd kept as insurance against future need after the worry of paying for the maypole ribbons. But now I didn't give a hang about future need; I was entirely caught up in the joy of giving. I retrieved three pennies from my hoard, ran to the shop and bought a meringue. I carried it home carefully, in a puffed up paper bag with plenty of air inside so that the meringue wouldn't get crushed. I made Mother's favourite egg sandwiches with thin brown bread and butter then, with sandwiches and cake on a tray, I went round to the shop.

Mother was serving a customer, so I put the tray on the table in the back room. I didn't stay to see her reaction to my gift; I decided to steal away, like the good fairy, so that Mother would have a lovely surprise.

I could hardly wait for her to come home when the shop closed. At last I heard the back door open and the plonk of her tray on the kitchen table. I was in there like a shot.

The first thing I saw was the meringue. Mother hadn't touched it! She turned from hanging her coat behind the door. Her eyes were bleak. She jerked her head at the meringue. 'What's that in aid of?'

'It's for you,' I said uncertainly.

'Oh, is it,' she sniffed. 'Well, I don't want it. You can't buy my love.'

I was too shocked for words. This couldn't be happening. What did she mean? I hadn't wanted to buy anything, only to give – to show that I wanted us to be friends. Then I realised: Mother had seen the meringue as a bribe. No such thought had entered my head, but her contempt made me feel that I had done something utterly shameful. Sick at heart I turned away. I had finished trying to get near Mother.

I didn't eat the rejected meringue: it would have choked me. I gave it to Dad; he enjoyed it, so that was a consolation.

School was better than being at home. I enjoyed most lessons, but I was finding it difficult to read writing on the blackboard. One day a teacher noticed me screwing up my eyes; she sent me to the clinic, where my eyes were tested and I was given a pair of glasses.

I was amazed by the new clarity of my vision, but I did not like my ugly wire-framed glasses; especially as Eddie Ashworth, who lived next door to us, kept jeering at me, 'Yah! Specky four-eyes.' I longed to retaliate with a rude name, but I couldn't think of one bad enough for him. Then, thanks to my dad, I found a corker.

On my birthday, Dad gave me a bible. I was far from thrilled, but he said, 'If you read your bible from the beginning to the end, I will give you a shilling.'

I had lost interest in beautiful character development and reverted to my usual badly behaved self, so perhaps Dad hoped that that some of the bible might rub off on me and improve my behaviour.

Well, I would have done anything for a shilling, so, that night in bed, I opened my bible and got started on Genesis. I soon got bogged down in the boring 'begat' lists of umpteen generations of fathers and sons, but I conscientiously read every word to honestly earn my shilling. I ploughed on till I reached the Book of Samuel in which Israelites and Philistines 'smote' each other in battle and hurled insults. The Israelites called their enemies 'uncircumcised Philistines'. I had no idea what that meant, so I went downstairs to Dad. He said that the Israelites had a custom called 'circumcision', but the Philistines didn't follow it, so they were uncircumcised. He didn't say what the custom was, so I wasn't much wiser. But that bit of biblical name-calling fascinated me. I thought 'uncircumcised Philistine' sounded vastly superior to 'Specky four-eyes,' so I decided to smite Eddie Ashworth with it at the first opportunity.

My chance came the very next day. I was in our back garden when Eddie climbed up on to the dividing wall. He stuck his thumbs in his ears, waggled his fingers derisively, crossed his eyes and stuck out his tongue. I let rip in triumph, 'Yah! You uncircumcised Philistine!'

Oh, heck! His mother's astonished face rose above the wall. 'Did you say that?'

I thought fast and pointed to the back street from where children's voices could be heard. But Eddie put the finger on me. She went straight to my dad, so I knew that what I had called Eddie must be something absolutely awful. I was certainly going to be in trouble with Dad. But he only told me, 'You'd better leave bible-reading until you are a bit older.' (He must have wished that he'd never started me on it.) I was glad to be rid of all the begetting and battling, but I regretted the loss of my shilling. However, I didn't lose out altogether. Dad treated me to a two-penny ice cream wafer that, he said, was only fair because I had read 'two penn'orth of the bible'.

By now I was completely hooked on *Flash Gordon*. On Saturdays, when I had done various jobs to Mother's satisfaction, I was given three pence, which paid for a matinee ticket and left a penny for sweets. But there was a problem: I could never be sure of getting my three pence.

I hated the dirty Saturday morning tasks of black-leading the fireplace and cleaning the cutlery with metal polish, jobs which made my hands black and smelly. Potato peeling came next. There were no washed vegetables then, so scraping off mud and peel was done on a newspaper; though why it couldn't have been done in a bowl of water, goodness knows.

When Mother started finding fault with my work, usually because I had left some of the eyes in the potatoes or smears on the fire-grate, I retaliated with cheek such as, 'And when could I ever do anything right for you?'

This resulted in, 'Right, lady; you've muckied your ticket,' which meant that I had lost my three pence and Flash Gordon. Even for him, I couldn't keep my big mouth shut.

I lost my hero for good when Auntie Edna told Mother that her Margaret was having music and elocution lessons. Not to be outdone by her in-laws, Mother promptly arranged for Margaret and me to have the same on Saturday afternoons, so it was goodbye to Flash Gordon for me. We also had to join a percussion band, which I hated. We banged away on drums, cymbals and triangles and made an appalling din. All I wanted was to go to a dancing class and join the Tower Children's Ballet. But entertaining summer visitors in the Tower Ballroom was not, in Mother's view, a cultural activity. Anyway, it all came to an end with the usual end-of-summer-season inability to pay two rents; we moved back to the shop and there was no money to spare for cultural activities.

Dad was still struggling to keep his shop going. Everyone was hard up. Customers who had bought furniture on hire purchase in the season of plenty now failed to pay their weekly instalments.

Every evening, after the shop closed, Dad pedalled off on his bike in the hope of collecting payments from defaulting customers. His knocks on their doors were seldom answered.

One evening he got home soaking wet after a fruitless ride in pouring rain. I heard him tell Mother how a woman in one house had wept because she couldn't pay the six pence she owed and, what was worse, she had no food to give to her hungry children. Dad said, 'I gave her six pence to buy bread.'

'Oh, yes,' Mother said bitterly. 'You can go round giving money away while I'm struggling to feed six of us.'

Dad protested that he had only given the six pence that he normally put in the collection box at church on Sundays. But Mother had a point; it must have been hard for her. One day she sent me to the Co-op butcher for 'two pennyworth of meat for the cat'. It was news to me that we had a cat, but off I went. The butcher, vast in his blue and white striped apron and straw hat, gave me a long look when I asked for cat meat. Then he wrapped up a generous handful of stewing meat, which had certainly not come out of the bucket into which inferior odds and ends of meat were cast. Nor was it the only occasion on which, thanks to that kind butcher, we had beef stew for our dinner.

Meanwhile, I too was having problems. At school I had moved up into Miss Wilton's class. She was absolutely terrifying, far worse than Miss Dobson who had her good points. Miss Wilton had none. She was a trap-faced martinet with lank, greasy hair and she was built like a tank. She plunged her way around the school with her head thrust forward at an aggressive angle, one eye twitching ferociously as she bellowed at us to get moving into her classroom.

She had no favourites – she hated all of us equally and I hated and feared her. I found it impossible to learn anything when I was sitting raw-nerved and quivering, waiting for her wrath to descend on me, which it often did, especially during arithmetic lessons.

I was (and I still am) a mathematical dunce, so, after Miss Wilton had marked our arithmetic, I was frequently made to stand in front of the class and work out the sums I had got wrong (which was all of them) on the blackboard, with the class looking on and Miss Wilton jeering as I chalked figures, rubbed them out and put them somewhere else in the hope that something would emerge to pacify her. Of course it never did.

It was all making my life a misery, so I took my problem to Dad. I asked him, 'When you went to school, were you good at sums?'

'No, I wasn't.' He was typing out a sermon for one of the Sunday services he was conducting whilst our minister was on holiday. He stopped typing and gave me his full attention, so I asked what he did when he couldn't get his sums right. He said, 'I prayed and asked God to help me.'

'Did He?' I was intrigued.

'Oh, yes. Prayers are always answered,' he assured me. Then he went on to say that prayers weren't always answered in the way you expected, because God moved in mysterious ways.

I wasn't entirely convinced that praying would work for me. I knew that nothing short of a miracle could make me good at sums, but, as there were plenty of miracles in the bible, I thought it was worth a try. That night I prayed, 'Please, God, make me good at sums.' It seemed a lot to ask, even of God, so I added, 'If you can't make me good at sums, could you please get Miss Wilton moved to another class?' Well, Dad was certainly right about God's mysterious ways: it wasn't Miss Wilton that got moved to another class, it was me.

I was demoted from the A stream to Miss Kilburn's B class. No doubt this was because I daily so dreaded going to school that I had stopped trying to do well at anything and got poor results in end of term tests. I stayed in Miss Kilburn's class for the rest of my time at Revoe, so I never got into Miss Callahan's scholarship class.

At first I was just relieved to have escaped Miss Wilton's tyranny; but Miss Kilburn turned out to be a dreary teacher. She accepted good or poor work with equal apathy; which was probably why she was in charge of those destined to fail the scholarship examination.

Once you were in a B class, your future education prospects were blighted because you had very little chance of passing the scholarship and going on to the grammar school. You were not expected or encouraged to pass, because it was assumed that you would fail. An occasion that illustrates this state of affairs has stuck in my mind. During an arithmetic lesson, Miss Kilburn introduced our class to fractions. At the conclusion of the lesson she put down her chalk, dusted her hands and said, 'Of course this is work the scholarship class is doing, so you girls don't need to worry too much about it.'

Of course I cannot claim that I would have passed had I been in the scholarship class, but I might have had a better chance. As it was, I and everyone in my class failed. There were two papers: for one you had to write an adventure story; I managed that all right. But the other paper required answers to sixty sums, most of which were totally incomprehensible to me.

In the autumn of 1938, along with the rest of my class, I went to Tyldesley Elementary school where, for the first time, we were introduced to current affairs.

Each morning at assembly, our headmistress, Miss Cooper, kept us up-to-date with events. With the aid of a wall map, she showed us how Adolph Hitler, the German dictator, had marched his troops into Austria, then into Czechoslovakia. She said that Hitler's invasion of other peoples' territories would have to be stopped or we would be next. And so we learned that the storm clouds of war were gathering.

Chapter 8

I didn't realise how the prospect of war was affecting people, especially my dad, until just before Remembrance Day. My teacher, Miss Farrar, told our class that we all had to support the British Legion's poppy sales because the money was used to help men who had been maimed for life during the Great War; so we must all come to school wearing a poppy on Remembrance Day.

Normally I never asked for money for anything, but when Miss Farrar told you to do something you did it, or else! So I asked Dad if I could have a penny for a poppy.

'No, you can't!' he said sharply.

'But, Dad!' I wailed. 'Miss Farrar says we've all got to wear a poppy to school on Remembrance Day. What'll I tell her?'

'Tell her I gave my blood!' he said fiercely.

I knew what he meant. Once he'd shown me and Margaret the scar from a bullet he'd got in his chest during the Battle of the Somme in the Great War. We had listened appalled as he told us how he'd crawled, bleeding, to where one of his mates lay badly wounded and crying, 'Will you, for God's sake, shoot me!"

Margaret and I, overcome with grief and horror, had run to the kitchen and wept into the roller towel. But now all I cared about was getting a poppy, so that I would not be in trouble with Miss Farrar. Besides, I wanted to be the same as my classmates.

On Remembrance Day, a poppy glowed on every chest

in the class, except mine. I could only hope that Miss Farrar wouldn't notice my lack but, after she'd marked the register, her eagle eye swept over the class and stopped at me.

'Betty, where's your poppy?'

If I'd had any sense I would have glanced down at my chest and cried, 'Oh! I've lost it.' But I was too worked up and embarrassed to think fast. I said the first thing that came into my head: 'My dad says he gave his blood, Miss.'

'Oh, does he indeed!' she said icily. The class tittered and I flushed with shame.

I was cross with Dad for causing me embarrassment so, when I got home, I told him what had happened; he was very sorry. He said, 'Your teacher wouldn't understand why I wouldn't let you buy a poppy.' Then he went on to tell me why he had refused.

'In 1914, we were promised that if we went to war we would be fighting the war to end all wars, and our sons and their sons would never have to fight. So we went willingly and trusted that the promise would be kept.

'But now, there's going to be another war, and all the thousands who gave their lives in the war to end wars are going to be betrayed. So Remembrance Day is a mockery of lives thrown away for nothing. And I won't buy red poppies because they represent useless bloodshed.'

'But it wasn't all for nothing,' I said. 'You won the war.'

'Nobody wins war,' he said bitterly.

During the following months there were many grim faces amongst the adults. Many feared that a war would put an end to holidays and their only source of income; this would be a disaster for landladies like my aunties as well as people who worked on The Pleasure Beach, the Promenade's Golden Mile, the piers and in many other branches of entertainment.

The prospect of future unemployment badly affected trade, so now Dad was having a desperate battle to keep his shop going. He put a notice in the window: 'All lino laid free of charge.' This brought a few customers. On Saturday afternoons I helped Dad to lay lino. My job was to stand on the edge of the roll of lino to stop it from curling up; then Dad cut it with a curved knife blade heated on a kitchen gas jet.

Lino was often laid in bedrooms where there was a great deal of dust under the beds. It gave Dad asthma attacks. I would stand, watching helplessly as he crawled round the floor, cutting, fitting and gasping for breath. He later told me that his asthma had started when he came home from the Great War suffering from shell shock. It plagued him for the rest of his life; especially when he was stressed, as he certainly was at that time. Free lino laying wasn't enough to keep the shop going, so he began to look for a job. But, with so much unemployment, there was nothing to be found.

Then, after Christmas, Mrs Brammer's father-in-law gave Dad a job in the small slipper mill he owned, which was near to our shop.

Mr Brammer and Dad were deacons of our church, so they often discussed church affairs when Mr Brammer called at the shop on his way to the mill. I didn't like him. He was the archetypal church patriarch, with fierce grey eyes beneath beetling bushy eyebrows. Totally committed to fighting the devil and all his works, he was always on the lookout for sin and sinners amongst the church members. Anyone he caught offending God was promptly and publicly castigated, as I was, one Sunday morning, when he caught me upsetting God in church.

I always sat with the other children in the front pews, then, when our part of the service was over and the others had gone home, I went up the aisle to sit with Dad at the back of the church for the rest of the service. One morning I ran up the aisle. Mr Brammer stepped out of his pew, grabbed my arm, and, in front of the congregation, told me off for 'running in God's house'. He said I must remember in future that the church was 'sacred ground'. I wished it would open and swallow me up.

Even Dad got the wrath of God via Mr Brammer when, one day, he was caught indulging in sinful pleasure. He was standing on a crowded station platform, peacefully smoking his pipe as he waited for his train, when suddenly Mr Brammer appeared on the opposite platform. He shouted across the lines, 'Edward Gibson! How long has the Devil had your soul?' So now, whenever he saw Mr Brammer coming, poor Dad quickly hid his smouldering pipe and caught it from Mother for burning holes in his pockets.

However, the other church members were not killjoys always ranting on about the Devil. Old Mr Brammer was an exception; perhaps his ferocious determination to fight the Devil was the result of an upbringing subject to Victorian hell-fire preaching. Anyway, I must not be too hard on him; he was kind at heart. Not only did he give Dad a job, he helped Mother. She looked after the shop when Dad was at the mill, so Mr Brammer told her that if she got a customer for anything she couldn't handle, such as unrolling a heavy carpet, she must ring up the mill and Dad would be allowed to go to her aid – which was a very thoughtful and kind concession.

Work at the slipper mill finished at noon on Saturdays. At the end of Dad's first week, I went to meet him. A man sweeping the yard took me up some stairs to the Clicking Room where Dad was working. He was standing at a bench with several men; they were cutting soles out of sheets of leather. I watched fascinated as their small knives whisked dexterously round metal-edged templates. Contact between knives and templates produced sharp clicks which, Dad said, was why the process was called clicking. As he was new to the work, he couldn't go as fast as the other men; he had to go carefully because a slip of the sharp knife could result in a badly cut finger.

A whistle blew and work stopped. I was helping the men to sweep up when Mr Brammer appeared. 'I can see you're not frightened of work,' he told me. 'When you leave school, I'll give you a job.' I was delighted.

'I wish I was old enough to start now,' I said as Dad and I walked home. He told me that I would not enjoy working in a slipper mill. 'Don't you like clicking?' I asked.

'No, I don't, I'm grateful for the job, but it's boring; I'm doing the same thing, hour after hour, day after day.' He was right about that, as I was later to discover, though not in Mr Brammer's mill.

It wasn't long before Mother announced that she wasn't going to look after the shop and do the housework, so I must do it. I wouldn't have minded doing my share of bedroom cleaning etc. but, as usual, Margaret got away with doing nothing. 'Why does it always have to be me?' I demanded furiously. 'Why can't Margaret do some of the work?'

'Because I've told you to do it,' Mother snapped.

Margaret smirked with satisfaction and mouthed, 'So there!' at me. By now she was well aware that her place in the family pecking order was superior to mine. Her attitude towards me had begun to reflect Mother's, which is hardly surprising considering the example she'd been set although, to be fair, Margaret was probably getting her own back for the way in which I made myself top dog by bossing her about when Mother wasn't there. All the same, when Mother and Margaret united in treating me as an inferior house skivvy, I was filled with resentment. They made me feel that I was only there to be made use of.

Furthermore, from my observation of relatives' and friends' households, I was becoming increasingly aware that our family wasn't right. A child can quickly sense when all is well within a family, so I had begun to envy those in which there was a warm atmosphere and everyone was loved and accepted. I yearned to be part of a family like that – a real family. I had never heard of compensation, but somehow I found it: I gave myself an imaginary ideal family.

My fantasy-parents were just warm presences. I didn't give them faces or talk to them but, every night in bed, I gave myself the immense pleasure of being their much-loved daughter. I made myself an only child because only ones got all their parents' attention as well as things which my parents could not afford to provide, so a lot of wish-fulfilment came into it. I gave myself a lifestyle based on that which I imagined was enjoyed by Shirley Temple, the child film star, with whom my friends and I would gladly have changed places had we been given the chance.

For my wardrobe, I selected Shirley Temple dresses that barely covered matching knickers; they were greatly envied by girls who, like me, wore dresses below the knees to allow for growth. Parties and dancing lessons were included; school was not.

Much as I revelled in dancing and dressing up, by far the most enjoyable part of my fantasy-life came at the end of my nightly sessions, when I created various scenarios that brought me into close contact with parental love and care. They were bound into something that I had always longed for but could never hope to have.

I had often watched glossy black horses trotting along the Promenade, drawing visitors sitting in elegant open landaus, whose gold and black wheel spokes turned and twinkled in the sunshine. In a fantasy world you can have anything you like, so now I rode in a landau every night. Wrapped in a velvet cloak, I sat between my parents; their arms were round me, holding me close as we rode along the Promenade. And, as it was dark, I added the sparkling spectacle of the Blackpool Illuminations for our mutual enjoyment.

Sometimes I changed this ending for a dramatic episode in which I was kidnapped by a witch who ill-treated me and made me scrub endless floors, until I was rescued by my parents who bore me away in a snowstorm. The final scene, with the storm raging outside the closed landau, was the most satisfying of all. It gave me a wonderful sense of security as I sat, protected from the elements, safe from the witch and cocooned in parental love. My fantasies were a great comfort to me, so I daily looked forward to my nights of happiness in the dream world.

Meanwhile, in the real world, despite the threat of war, everything seemed to go on as usual until a terrible disaster struck. It was the result of preparation for war.

On 1 June 1939, the world's newest and most modern submarine, the Royal Navy's *Thetis*, sailed to make her maiden dive in Liverpool Bay. On board were 103 men; they all expected to be back on shore in time for tea. The dive took place but something went wrong: *Thetis* was unable to resurface.

After the news that she was in trouble was broadcast on the wireless, everyone waited in agonised expectation. Then hopeful news came: four members of the crew had got out through the escape chamber. Hope was dashed when no more men emerged. It was feared that a fifth man had got jammed and blocked the escape exit so no one else could get out. The remaining men had only thirty-six hours left until they ran out of air.

The next morning, during school assembly, we prayed for the men whose time was swiftly running out. We sang:

> Eternal Father strong to save
> Whose arm doth bind the restless wave,
> Oh, hear us when we cry to thee
> For those in peril on the sea.

Whenever I hear that hymn now, I think of those trapped

sailors and the desperate hours of waiting and hoping that they and their families endured.

Wireless bulletins reported the progress of the rescue attempt being made by ships stationed above *Thetis*. Divers passed a stout wire cable beneath the stricken vessel. The hopes of the men inside must have risen when they heard the grating and grinding of the wire. The ships hauled on the wire; slowly *Thetis* began to rise. At one point her stern could actually be seen above the water – there was a photograph of it in the evening paper – then suddenly the cable snapped and *Thetis* went back to the bottom. With only a few hours of air left, those poor men must have known that their last chance of rescue had gone.

Their time ran out and the nation mourned with the families of the ninety-nine lost men. Ten thousand people attended a memorial service held outside Liverpool's Town Hall. The four survivors were there; it was later reported that one of them had had his pay withheld because he couldn't produce his pay book: it was at the bottom of the sea. Also present at the service was another crewmember who might well have shared the fate of the ninety-nine; but, on the day, *Thetis* sailed he'd gone to his mother's funeral, so, ironically, her death had probably saved his life.

The loss of *Thetis* stays in my mind as the start of all that was to come with millions of lives lost at sea, in the air and on land. But in the early summer of 1939, war still lay in the future.

Blackpool was full of visitors enjoying themselves, seemingly without a care in the world. But there was anxiety; I saw it surface amidst the hectic whirling gaiety of The Pleasure Beach. It was near to our church, so, after Sunday school, I often went to The Beach and made straight for La Celeste's booth. I never missed going to see her amazing performances, which were a taste of what could be marvelled at inside the booth on payment of six pence. The free show more than contented me. La Celeste fascinated me from the moment she appeared on the stage outside the booth in her purple velvet cloak and glittering tiara. She sat at a table on which there was a crystal ball. Then the barker described her amazing mystic power of seeing into the future. Actually, she didn't look very mystical; perhaps she was trying to look remote and mysterious, but she looked thoroughly bored, which rather detracted from the barker's efforts. But I wasn't put off by how she looked; I hung on her every word because she was absolutely amazing.

That day when I joined the crowd in front of the stage, the performance followed the usual pattern, with blindfolded La Celeste identifying various articles held up by the audience. She even gave the dates on coins and she was never wrong. The blindfold was removed; then the barker said that La Celeste would now look into her crystal ball and answer any questions the audience asked. There were various queries of a personal nature such as, 'Will I get married?' and 'Will I have to have an operation?'

Then a male voice shouted from the back of the crowd, 'Is there going to be a war?'

'No,' said La Celeste. 'There is not going to be a war.' There was a buzz of relief and a woman cried, 'Thank God!'

I ran home and told Dad the good news. I thought he'd be delighted, but he wasn't. He said La Celeste was a fraud, adding, 'Only God knows what the future holds.'

Preparation for war was certainly going ahead. It even disrupted our school's timetable. For hours we ran wild in the playground whilst the staff sat in conclave with Miss Cooper. They must have been discussing what was to be done in the case of air raids. One morning, Miss Cooper announced that we were to run home as fast as we could, then report back to school the time taken to reach home. She said it was an experiment to find out whether, in the event of an air raid warning, we would have enough time reach our homes before any trouble (we knew she meant bombing) started. Sending us home was probably all that our worried motherly headmistress could devise for our safety until underground shelters could be provided in the school's playground.

'What's going on?' Dad asked when I shot into the house and checked the time on the clock. I explained and he said, 'If anything happened I'd run to school to get you, so don't worry.' I wasn't worried. I was enjoying the heady upside-down feeling of everything being excitingly different. Nor was I the only one to hope that there would be a war. My friends and I thought that war meant we could go on enjoying all the excitement as well as our extra playtime during the now almost daily staff meetings. In the light of future events, they were probably debating how the school would cope with an influx of evacuees should war be declared.

Chapter 9

War seemed very likely to happen because, soon after schools broke up for the August holiday, we were all issued with gas masks and evacuees began to arrive. I remember seeing groups of scruffy children trailing round the streets behind billeting officers. The children had labels tied to their ragged coats as if they were parcels being delivered at doors.

Blackpool took evacuees from Salford – in those days a slum area. It was said that Blackpool learned more about Salford in one week than it had learned in twenty years.

Many of the children were filthy, and most were undernourished and in poor health. Their hosts complained of lice, dirty habits and bed-wetting. Sheets had to be washed every day and there were no washing machines then. Certainly people had had no idea of what they would be taking on when they agreed to provide a safe haven for the evacuees. (The condition of poor people living in slum areas, so shockingly revealed by the evacuation, did in fact lead to post-war social reform with free access to medical care, better housing and family allowances.)

On 1 September 1939, Hitler invaded Poland. Britain and France had promised to back up Polish resistance. Hitler was warned that if he did not withdraw his troops by midday on Sunday, 3 September, then Britain and France would go to war against Germany.

The following day, I went to the Saturday matinee at the

Empire cinema. School was due to start on Monday, so it was the end of holiday freedom. But we got a surprise!

After the Mickey Mouse cartoon ended, words suddenly appeared on the screen: 'All schools are closed until further notice.'

There was a moment of electrified silence as we took it in, then up went a tremendous cheer. 'Hurraaaay!' we yelled. It was a wonder the roof didn't fly off.

Of course, our jubilation was not shared by the adults, who waited, fearfully hoping that Hitler would agree to withdraw.

On Sunday morning, Dad and I went to church. Naturally he expected that our minister would pray for peace, but he didn't; he prayed for the King and for 'the triumph of right over might (our victory) in the coming conflict'. Dad was appalled but hardly surprised. He wasn't keen on our newly appointed, university-educated young minister who, Dad said, preached above people's heads. I remember an example of this quoted by Dad: 'Ah, brethren, consider the inexhaustible resources of the human soul.'

Anyway, that Sunday morning the congregation had to consider an exhaustive examination of the letters of St. Paul, despite the fact that everyone was anxious to get home in time for Prime Minister Chamberlain's midday broadcast on the wireless.

On our way home, Dad said, 'If I'd been taking that service there would have been no sermon. I would have called everyone to come and sit together in the front pews, then we would have prayed for peace.'

By the time we got home, Mr Chamberlain had told the nation that, as no word had been received from Hitler, we were now at war with Germany. Dad went upstairs, fetched his Great War campaign medals and threw them in the dustbin.

One Saturday, the town's cinema screens announced: All schools will reopen on Monday. Of course everyone yelled, 'Booooo!' But, when we got back to school, we again found things excitingly different. We now shared our school with some evacuees, so we had our lessons in the mornings and the evacuees had theirs in the afternoons, whilst we were taken to the beach to paddle in the sea and play ball games. The weather was still warm and sunny.

In an attempt to keep up the normal timetable, our lesson times were halved: twenty minutes instead of forty for each subject. This was further reduced by the time taken moving between classrooms, so not a great deal of work got done.

Another disruption was donning our gas masks for part of a lesson. This was so that we could get used to wearing them should there be a gas attack. We couldn't stop laughing at the sight of a room full of weird masked faces; and we naughtily annoyed our teachers by blowing through the rubber sides of our masks and making rude fart noises. You had to carry your gas mask in its cardboard case on a shoulder string everywhere you went; if you arrived at school without it, you were promptly sent home to fetch it and given detention after school.

Despite the fun we were having, life wasn't all roses. Before long my friends and I were living in terror of the evacuees, who lurked round corners and fell upon us with cries of, 'Bash the buggers!'

They were not all bullies. Jack, who was billeted with one of our neighbours, became my friend. He was a lively cheerful lad, who swore as naturally as he breathed. I was quite fascinated by his bad language, which, incidentally, was not used in a belligerent way: it was merely a sort of exclamation that preceded almost every sentence he uttered. It wasn't long before I learned what his life was like in Salford.

We were both keen collectors of cigarette cards that we picked up from empty cigarette packets on the streets, or got from people whom we saw smoking. The cards had pictures on one side and information on the other; so we learned about wild flowers, butterflies, railway engines, ships, flags and many other aspects of our world. My interest in history was sparked off by the red-gold hair and jewelled crowns of the Plantagenet and Tudor monarchs.

To get a complete set of a series, you swapped cards with other children. One day Jack and I were sitting on our coalhouse roof swapping cards when my dad came out with a shovel to get some coal. He stopped for a friendly chat with Jack, then he gave us a penny each for ice cream. After he'd gone, Jack said, 'Was that your dad?'

'Yes,' I said casually, as I shuffled through my cigarette cards.

'I wish 'e was my dad,' Jack said longingly.

'Why?' I looked at him in surprise. 'Haven't you got a dad?'

'Yeah,' he said bitterly. 'I've gorra right bugger. 'E belts 'ell out o' me an' I'm glad "e's inside.'

'Inside?' I queried.

'The nick… prison.'

I was dumbfounded. I didn't say any more, but what Jack had said left a lasting impression on me. Even now I wonder what became of him. Perhaps he was one of those evacuees for whom removal from a bad environment brought great change for the better. Jack's swift response to my dad's kindly interest showed his ability to recognise that there was something to be desired that was better than what he had. All he needed to rise above his deprivation was caring guidance; I hope he got it.

The following Sunday morning, after church service, two lads from the Young Men's Fellowship told Dad that they'd been called up. They were very excited at the prospect of fighting the Germans, but Dad was very upset. He often spoke at Fellowship meetings, so he knew all the lads and was interested in their welfare. 'They've got no idea what war is like,' he told me as we walked home. 'But I was just the same when I was their age. When the Great War started I cried to my mother to let me join up. She gave way in the end; but when I found out what war was like, I cried to go home.

'It was awful in the trenches; lads I'd grown up with were killed. After I was wounded, I was in a field hospital ward with some of my mates. We all knew that as soon as we recovered we'd be sent back to the trenches. We were terrified; we knew we'd be killed, so we ripped the stitches out of our wounds to stop them healing.'

'Oh, no!' I cried.

'Yes, we did. But they patched us up and sent us back.'

'Did you kill any Germans?' I asked.

He took his pipe out of his pocket and stopped to light it. He took a long time to get it going then, as we walked on, he began telling me what had happened when he got the terrible news that his brother, Alec, had been killed. 'I got drunk,' he said. 'I started shouting "I'll kill every bloody German I see".'

I was stunned. I could hardly believe that my dad had got drunk and used bad language. 'I've never had another drink from that day to this,' he said, 'and I didn't carry out my drunken threat to kill. I was alone on guard when I saw a German wandering about on No Man's Land. I levelled my rifle and shouted, Hands up! He flung his arms up and ran off yelling, "Kamerad! Kamerad!" I let him go. I didn't want to kill him. He was some mother's son.'

'But he might have killed you!' I gasped.

'Then I wouldn't be here and neither would you.' That puzzled me.

I said, 'How could you getting killed have stopped me from being here?'

'Well,' he said, 'you couldn't be here if I hadn't survived; you see, I had a share in your creation.'

I didn't see. 'What—?' But Dad cut me off with, 'I'll tell you when you are twenty-one.' It was his usual reply to questions he wasn't going to answer, so I gave up. But I wondered...

It must seem incredible now that, at the age of twelve, I didn't know the so-called 'facts of life'. Nowadays quite young children are clued up on every aspect of sex; much of their knowledge appears to be gained from television. It was different for my generation: there was no television, and sex and procreation were shrouded in mystery. Various absurd explanations were given to children who asked where babies came from: under gooseberry bushes was one place in which they could be found; they could also be brought by a stork. You could even buy a baby at the Co-op!

At least the story Dad told me when I was little showed more imagination. I had never tired of hearing how, one dark night, I had floated down from Heaven in a snowstorm, crying because I was cold, and Dad had caught me in a warm blanket.

I now knew that it wasn't true because, when my brother John was born, Dad had told me, 'Babies don't really float down from Heaven; they come from mothers.' The shop's bell had saved him from further explanation but, at that time, I don't remember wanting to know more. I did now, but Dad had said I must wait, so I couldn't ask.

However, I soon forgot all that in the events that were soon to follow.

Dad came home early from the mill and told us, 'There's a shortage of orders, so we've all been put on half-time.' I knew that this was very serious indeed because, with trade at rock bottom due to the outbreak of war, his mill wage was almost our family's only means of support. Nor was that the only worry.

Dad told Mother, 'I've got a shop full of furniture I can't sell; there'll be a bill for it from Simpsons any day now. I don't know what we're going to do.'

She said, 'We must get out of Blackpool… Take the business somewhere else.'

For several days they discussed where they might go; then Mother's elder sister, Auntie Maggie, arrived from Nelson, where her husband and a son worked in the cotton mills. She often came to stay for a few days and her visits always put Mother in a good mood. They were very different: Auntie was plump and placid, Mother thin and discontented, but they were very fond of each other.

Auntie listened as Mother told her that the shop was in a bad way. 'We've got to leave Blackpool,' she said, 'but we don't know where to go.'

Dad added, 'Anyway, we can't be sure that trade would be better somewhere else.'

Auntie said, 'Well, there's plenty of brass in Nelson. Your shop would do all right there, and you could come and live near me.'

Mother was delighted; but Simpson's bill had arrived, so Dad was reluctant to move until it was paid.

'And how's that going to happen while we're stuck here?' Mother demanded.

'I don't know,' he said. 'I'll just have to pray for help.'

'A fat lot of good that'll do,' Mother retorted, and Auntie went home disappointed.

The next day, when I got home from school, Uncle Lennie was there. Normally he came to Blackpool only in August, so I was overjoyed by this unexpected visit. After tea, Uncle and Dad settled down for a chat. I was washing up in the kitchen, but stretching my ears as usual. I heard Uncle tell Dad, 'I can let you have a few hundred, interest free of course.'

Dad must have felt that Uncle was the answer to his prayers. He settled his Simpsons debt and arrangements began for our move to Nelson. The only problem was that, after we'd moved, Dad would not be able to collect the hire purchase instalments still outstanding. He arranged for a nephew to collect the payments for which he was to be paid a small commission. Unfortunately this was to end when the nephew was called up for army service. As far as I know, most of the HP money was never repaid!

I went to say goodbye to my aunties and cousins. I wasn't too sad, because all of my aunties said that I must stay with them for holidays.

As it turned out, it was a pity that we didn't stay where we were. But neither my parents nor anyone else knew that, before long, it was to be boom-time for Blackpool. The area became a training centre for various branches of the armed forces, mostly RAF, with personnel based in camps and boarding houses all the year round, and trade benefited from the influx.

We left the shop for the last time, with Mother and Dad full of high hopes. It was early in November when we arrived in Nelson. Compared to Blackpool it was a drab, dreary place with a forest of smoking mill chimneys and rows of stone-built houses with front doors opening onto the street.

Auntie Maggie lived in one of them; it was on Every Street. She used to joke that she'd lived on 'every street in Nelson'. Actually, she was in a fair way to doing that, because, like Mother, she was always moving house. Maybe this compulsion was a family trait. But they moved for different reasons. Mother moved to get a better house, but Auntie's moves were often made to a house that was almost a replica of the one she'd moved out of. Margaret once asked her why she moved so often. Her answer was rather odd: 'If yer can't flit, yer shot at,' she said firmly.

We didn't live in a house like Auntie's. The small shop Dad rented on Railway Street had no living accommodation, so Mother found a rather superior house on a select road with a view of Pendle Hill in the distance.

I went to a senior school with Auntie's daughter. Cousin Bunty and I had been friends for as long as I could remember because she and Auntie had often stayed with us in Ilkley and Blackpool. Bunty and I were still good friends, despite the fact that I had often got her into trouble.

On one occasion, a few years back, I had suggested that we dress up as Hawaiian dancing girls – like the ones we'd seen in a film about Hawaii.

'But we haven't got grass skirts,' Bunty pointed out.

I was stumped for a moment, then I had a good idea. I checked that Dad was in the living room having a cup of tea; then I sneaked into the shop and cut a length off the orange lamp fringe that was sold by the yard. We danced naked, swaying the fringe round our skinny hips. This was followed by a bathe in a tropical lagoon – we had to make do with the bath. Unfortunately the fringe wasn't colourfast, so, when Mother and Auntie found us disporting in bright orange water, we got our orange-dyed bottoms smacked and my spending money was docked to pay for the fringe.

Bunty never minded when my good ideas went wrong, so she was delighted when I arrived in Nelson. She said, 'You'll be coming to my school, so we'll be in the same class.' I knew that that wasn't going to happen because I was a year older than Bunty.

On my first day she took me to the headmistress, a plump, elderly lady called Miss Long. She asked how old I was. I said I was twelve and Bunty asked if I could be in her class. 'But your class is for eleven-year-olds,' Miss Long said. Bunty pleaded that we were cousins. Miss Long smiled at us then she said, 'Oh, all right.'

I could hardly believe my ears! Nobody ever dreamed of asking to be put in a class of their own choice; headmistresses told you which class you were to be in. Of course, Bunty and I were overjoyed; at least I was at first, but I soon got fed up with that school. Most of the teachers were like Revoe's Miss Kilburn – uninspiring and dull. I wonder now, was the fact that children in a Nelson elementary school were destined for the cotton mills the reason for our teachers' indifference to our progress? Or was it that they lacked strong leadership?

Margaret was going to a junior school where she got homework because she was in a scholarship class. Her obvious enjoyment of school and her evening absorption in homework made me even more dissatisfied with my boring school; so perhaps I was seeking some stimulating response when I asked my teacher, Miss Pollard, for some homework. She told me to write a description of a lamppost.

I wasn't inspired by lampposts, so I decided to ask Dad for some ideas. After school, I set off for the shop. It was dark by then and the streets were unlit because of the wartime blackout regulations. I always took Dad's tea to the shop because he was staying open during the evenings, as he had in Blackpool. I told him about my lamppost problem; he pondered as he ate his marmite sandwiches, then said, 'Well, you could describe a lamppost as erect... immovable.'

Dad's help gave me an idea. When I got home I wrote a story about a lamppost called Lofty who, although no longer able to light the streets because of the blackout, still stood, erect and immovable, waiting for the War to end so that he could shine again. I gave my story to Miss Pollard; she put it in her desk and that was the last I saw or heard of my opus. Perhaps it wasn't a very good story, but at least it was topical.

The mills were busy with government contract production of textiles needed for the armed forces, so it was probably true that there was 'plenty of brass in Nelson'. But very little of it found its way into Dad's shop. Shopping time was governed by the mills' working hours. Most people worked in the mills, so shopping was done after they closed, at noon on Saturday. Furthermore, the onset of winter, early darkness and blacked-out streets with no shop windows lit didn't encourage people to spend much time or money on shopping. It was freezing cold; people wanted to get home to a warm fire, so shopping was confined to essentials such as food.

At that time of the year, a shop selling furniture and carpets was a non-starter, so Dad was again desperately worried. He told Mother that, with hardly any money coming in, he couldn't afford to hang on in the hope of better times in spring, especially as he had promised to repay Uncle's loan by monthly instalments.

He must have been praying for help but, ironically, the war that he'd hoped would never happen was his salvation. Many young men had been called up, so jobs were available for older men. The Pearl Assurance Company needed replacement agents. Dad was offered a choice of vacancies in several Lancashire towns; one was at Rawtenstall, in the Rossendale Valley. This was where Mother's brother lived and, as it was not far from Nelson, she and Auntie would still be near to each other; so of course our destination was never in doubt. The shop was closed and only a few weeks after we had arrived in Nelson, we left for Rawtenstall.

Chapter 10

It was snowing when we arrived in the Rossendale Valley in January 1940. On a previous one-day visit, when his appointment as a Pearl agent had been confirmed, Dad had found a house to rent. When Mother saw it, she was appalled. It was a mill worker's house, just like the ones in Nelson. In mill towns, streets of stone-built houses had been erected near the mills so that employees could live conveniently close to their work. There was a cotton mill with a tall chimney pouring out black smoke behind our house on Omerod Street.

Dad had taken the house because it was cheap to rent; he wanted to keep expenses as low as possible until his debt to Uncle was paid. All the rooms were very small, but it was quite a good house; we had a front room, a living room and a kitchen. Upstairs were two bedrooms and stairs to an attic. There was a bathroom, but, much to Mother's disgust, it hadn't got a lavatory. Dad said, 'There's a petty in the backyard.'

This was something new to us children. Margaret and I peered into the dark depths of a hole in a box seat filling the space between the whitewashed walls of the outhouse. We could hear water trickling far below. Suddenly there was a tremendous crash and a great noise of rushing water. We leapt back in terror, ran to Dad and told him that we were scared of the petty.

He explained to us how it worked. 'There's a tippler-tank at the bottom of the hole. When it's full of water, it tips over and washes everything into the sewer.'

'Where does the water come from?' I asked.

'All the house water from the kitchen and bathroom goes down a pipe into the tank.' He went on to tell us that, when he was a boy, they'd had an earth-midden in the back yard. 'There were no sewers then. Men used to come at night to empty the middens with long shovels.'

'That must have been a horrible job,' I gasped.

'It was. The middens didn't half stink; and there were flies galore in hot weather. So a tippler-tank would have seemed wonderful to us.' But our petty was never going to seem wonderful to me because I got the job of emptying the jerries (chamber pots) kept under our beds for night use.

After the removal men had gone, we were all ready for a cup of tea, so we began to search various cartons for the kettle. Suddenly there was a thump on the back door. Dad opened it and a small middle-aged lady carrying a tray of pint pots of tea came in. She said, 'You must be ready for a cupper.'

Dad cleared a space for the tray on the cluttered table. 'Thank you very much! It's very kind of you; we are certainly ready for a cupper, Mrs…'

'Evans. Edie Evans. I'm next door,' she jerked a thumb at the wall. 'If you want owt give me a shout.'

Mother hastily pulled herself together and invited Mrs Evans to sit down.

'Nay,' she said, 'I'm not stopping. My lass'll be in from t'mill for her tea. If you want summat to eat, there's a chip shop bottom o' t' brew.' Then she was gone.

'Well,' Dad said, as we drank our tea, 'we've certainly got a very kind neighbour.'

'What's a brew?' Edwina asked. Dad said it must be the local name for a hill, and so it was. Our street sloped steeply downhill to where the chip shop stood.

'Moved in up t' brew, 'ave you?' The proprietor grinned

at Dad and me as he wrapped up our parcel of fish and chips. People waiting to be served smiled at us and said, "Ow do.' As we walked home, Dad said, 'Everyone's very friendly. I think we're going to like living up t' brew.' I knew that Mother wasn't going to like it one bit, but I didn't say so because Dad was so happy.

I have never forgotten the smile on his face when he showed me his first pay envelope from the Pearl and said, 'I shall have this in my hand every week!' Freed from the worry of a failing business and assured of a regular income, his relief was enormous. He didn't even mind when he had to tramp through deep snow to collect premiums from hilltop farmers.

Meanwhile we all had to endure weeks of the intense cold of a Pennine winter, the like of which we had never seen in Blackpool, where there was never more that a light scattering of snow. In Rossendale it covered the landscape feet deep. If you walked on a pavement, an avalanche of snow could descend from a roof on to your head, so you walked in the road, cleared by snowploughs.

I enjoyed the new experience of sledging and snowballing, but my hands were frozen inside my sodden gloves. To warm up quickly, I stuck my hands in hot water. I never did it again. Oh, the agony of circulation too swiftly restored! How I danced and howled until the excruciating pain subsided. And I got chilblains on my toes. They itched and burned when I was in bed. Mrs Evans told me, 'Stick yer feet in t' jerry, luv, that'll cure chilblains.' Much as I loathed the idea, I was driven to try it, but it didn't work.

My new school was much better than my Nelson school. I even got some help with my maths problems. Miss Dodd kept me after school and patiently tried to make me understand the baffling movement of decimal points. I had always been scared of maths teachers, but I liked gentle

Miss Dodd, so I made up my mind to really try. I did my best to concentrate and listened intently to every word she said. Although I never really got the hang of decimals, Miss Dodd wrote on my term end report: 'Has attended well to her work.' That encouraging comment, the first I'd ever had for maths, gave me more satisfaction than all the high marks I got for subjects I was good at.

Mother didn't want to risk a change of school spoiling Margaret's chance of going to a grammar school; she had arranged for her to stay with Auntie Maggie during the week so that she could sit the scholarship examination at her Nelson school.

When she came home at weekends, we went round to our Cousin Millie's house, which was behind the ironmongery shop kept by Mother's brother, Uncle Arthur, and his wife, Auntie Libby.

Margaret and I adored sixteen-year-old Millie and vied with each other for her attention. She always had time for us. When the light evenings came, she took us walking on the hills. It was another new experience for us.

Millie wasn't the only reason we went to her house. We went because we could always be sure of a generous slice of Auntie Libby's homemade cake. Enormously fat and cheerful, she fed everybody in sight. I remember, one freezing day, seeing her take a bowl of hot broth to a man working down a hole in the road outside the house.

In addition to being the soul of kindness, Auntie was a wonderful source of entertainment; her dramatically told tales held Margaret and me enthralled.

I remember one about the death of her old cat. Its demise had presented Auntie with a very difficult problem. Normally dead cats and dogs were taken to a mill and cremated in the fire hole. Unfortunately the cat died during Wakes Week, the annual holiday, when all the mills were closed and the fires let out for boiler cleaning. Auntie hadn't got a garden, so she couldn't bury the cat (back yards were common to most local properties) so she decided to cremate it on her living room fire. This was the dramatic-horrific part of the tale. 'Eee!' she cried, throwing her hands in the air, 'you should've seen and smelt that cat rendering down. Its fat ran all over the hearth and onto the rug!' 'Rendering down' was the extraction of fat from meat to make dripping, so Uncle Arthur joked that they'd eaten the cat dripping on toast.

Mother was scathing about the cremation of the cat; she said that it was 'typical of Libby'. Sisters-in-law seldom found favour with Mother: in this case it was because she thought that Libby wasn't good enough for her brother. This puzzled me because I could see that, although Uncle Arthur was quiet compared with Auntie Libby, they suited each other.

When the shop was closed for half-day, they went by bus to Barley, their favourite Pennine village, where, after tea in a café, they went to a cinema in Burnley. In their mutual enjoyment of this and other simple pleasures, I sensed a contented togetherness that impressed me. And I loved being at their house, it seemed filled with warmth; unlike home, where Mother's discontent chilled everything and everybody.

Before long she put a card that read 'Dressmaker' in the front room window. No doubt she wanted to use her sewing skill to help pay off the debt to Uncle, then we could move to a modern house.

She was a very good dressmaker. As well as making new clothes for customers, she did very difficult renovation work. With wartime rationing, clothing coupons had been issued. People wanted to use their few coupons to buy something new for best, so they contrived ways to make do for everyday wear. They presented Mother with old coats to be transformed into boys' trousers or ladies' skirts and goodness knows what else. She often said that she would rather make six new garments than one renovation. But, all credit to her, she struggled on. Many orders came in, so she was very busy. I did the housework at weekends or in the evenings when I wasn't at the Baptist Sunday school, where there was plenty going on with socials and rehearsals for plays.

There were other activities of a more serious nature, which included classes for a scripture examination, with Dad as our teacher. We all passed because nobody ever got failed. I also went to 'Christian Endeavour' meetings, where I was required to take my turn at presenting a short service. This may sound a tall order for a thirteen-year-old, but I had only to read a prayer and tell a bible story in my own words. It was probably early training for Sunday school teaching. And I was a member of the 'Girls Auxiliary' where, as well as more hymns and prayers, we had discussions about how we might work to make a better world after the War.

But the end of the War was a long way off. That winter, the German air force started bombing our cities. Almost every night the rising-falling wail of the air-raid warning awoke us. Dad fixed up a shelter in the coal cellar. There was a camp bed for Edwina and John and stools for the rest of us. Mrs Evans was a widow, so Dad invited her and her seventeen-year-old daughter, Marion, to join us whenever there was a raid.

There we would all sit drinking tea and listening to the distant crump of bombs falling on Manchester. Our sash windows rattled with every detonation, so Dad put wedges inside the frames. When the all clear sounded its long note, we went back to bed. Sometimes we had just got off to sleep when the siren sent us back to the cellar. But our disrupted sleep was nothing compared to the death and destruction rained on our cities. Of course there was always the chance that a stray bomber driven away from Manchester by anti-aircraft fire could unload its bombs on Rossendale, but we were never bombed. Eventually the air raids stopped for a while, so I slept undisturbed in the attic that had been my room since the day we'd moved in. I loved my attic eyrie, where I could read in peace surrounded by cartons of oddments unneeded downstairs.

One day when I was cleaning the attic I lifted a heavy carton; the bottom gave way, the contents fell out and there on the floor was my Grandma's family bible! It must have been given to Dad after she had died.

Of course, I now knew the secret Grandma had said I mustn't know until I was older. I supposed that my unexpected request to look inside the bible must have startled Grandma into accidentally revealing the existence of the secret. I was glad now that it had, because her slip of the tongue had led to my discovery that I'd had a real mother whom I was sure would have loved me.

I examined the family record pages at the front of the bible, but, much to my surprise, there was nothing at all about me or my mother. In fact, the record ended shortly before I was born. I concluded that Grandma had forgotten she'd stopped keeping the record and thought that details of my birth and my mother's death had been entered.

It was some years later that I discovered why the record had not been kept up after my birth. On the day my mother died, Grandma had carried me home and looked after me until I was nearly two years old. At that time she was over sixty and had already reared eleven of her own children without the help of her alcoholic husband. Taking on yet another baby, as well as running her boarding house, must have been an exhausting struggle, so she certainly would not have had time to spare for keeping up the family record. But I am glad to record my gratitude for my valiant grandma's love and care for me.

I found many interesting items between the bible's pages. There were yellowed newspaper cuttings, reporting the deaths of young relatives killed in the 1914–18 war, and dried buttonhole flowers from long-ago weddings. Best of all was a small picture of Jesus standing beside a door and holding a glowing lantern (Holman Hunt's *The Light of the World*). On the back of the picture were some words that Grandma must have written when I was a baby: 'For my wee Betty.' All her love for me seemed to be in those words, so the picture became a treasured link with my grandma.

I was to wish that I had removed the picture and the other items because, after a future house move, the bible disappeared. I asked Mother whether she'd put it somewhere. She said disparagingly, 'Oh, it got thrown out.'

'Got thrown out!' I cried. 'You mean you threw it out.'

'Well, nobody wanted it,' she said uncomfortably.

'I wanted it. It was my grandma's bible,' I said furiously. But I had to accept its loss.

By the time the summer following the air raids came, Margaret had passed the scholarship and was back at home. During the August school holiday we played at cowboys and Indians with a group of local boys and girls, but this soon began to pall. We were all curious about the secrets of the adult world. We knew next to nothing about sex and procreation, so we decided to find out what we could and pool our knowledge. For this purpose we formed 'The Nature Club'. There was only one rule: you had to bring to each meeting a snippet of new information about the facts of life. We met in a den made from wooden packing cases left on a piece of spare ground near a mill and revealed our discoveries. In reality, there were no available sources of information and no one dreamed of asking parents, so what could not be obtained was frequently invented. The result was an extraordinary collection of rubbish, including the 'fact' that sexual union took place only to make a baby, so parents had done it according to the number of children they had produced. One of the boys said, 'Even the King and Queen must have done it twice, 'cos they've got two kids.' We were silent with awe at the thought of their majesties indulging in such undignified activities.

When the new term started I was in Mr Slater's pre-school leavers' class. He was a very good teacher so I enjoyed his lessons. One day, much to my embarrassment, he read out to the class the first composition I had written for him. He told me to see him after school. When the others had gone home I stood at his desk. Much to my surprise he said, 'Betty, what are you doing here? You should be at the grammar school.'

I said, 'But, Sir, I failed the scholarship. I can't do maths.' Of course he was well aware of that, but he smiled encouragingly and told me, 'Something could be done about that.' I'm sure that he would have been willing to tutor me. Nothing happened, but he must have contacted my parents. Several years later he told me, 'I tried to get you to the grammar school, but it was no use.'

Of course it was no use. At that time I was nearly fourteen; I would soon be starting work and my parents were relying on my wages to help pay off the debt. Furthermore, they could not have afforded to pay for me to go to the grammar school; you had to pay if you hadn't got a scholarship. Nor could they have afforded to buy two lots of uniform. I remember that Margaret, now at the grammar, had only one school blouse, which she had to wash and iron every evening.

My final months in school were mostly devoted to training in the domestic arts; this included taking my turn at making school dinners for a few children who lived on hill farms and couldn't get home for the midday meal.

A few days before I left school, Mr Slater produced an exercise book and told those of us who were leaving to write down the name of the place in which we were going to work. He peered over my shoulder and clicked his tongue in disgust as I wrote 'Riverside Footwear'. It was one of many Rossendale mills making slippers, boots, shoes and sandals. They were all called slipper mills because originally slippers had been their only product. In the nineteenth century, workers in the local felt mills had begun to fashion crude slippers using felt off-cuts. From these humble beginnings had come the first slipper mill and eventually a thriving industry.

Dad had got the job for me through a church member who was a boss at the Riverside mill. A church connection, in Dad's view, ensured my protection in the world of work.

Despite Mr Slater's disgust, I couldn't wait to start work. Mrs Evans' daughter, who worked in a slipper mill, had told me that, on piece work, the harder you worked the more you earned. And I was very keen indeed to earn lots of money to help Dad pay his debt.

Chapter 11

On my first day at the mill I followed the crowd of workers streaming into the mill's yard and through an immense door. Our feet beat a steady rhythmic tramp as we went, closely packed together, up and up flights of stone steps, before people turned off into different departments on each floor. I went up to the top floor, where I was to be a table-hand in the Closing Room where footwear uppers were made. It was also called the Girls' Room, although some of the girls were in their sixties.

It was a long room with sewing machine tables on one side and tables for handwork and inspection on the other. In the centre of the room was a desk at which the forewoman, Rita, stood. Tall, pale-faced and severe, she wore a crisp white cotton coat nipped in at her slim waist. She gave me a wintry smile, handed me over to a woman on the handwork table and told her to set me on 'buckling up'.

Ada, cheerful and motherly, gave me a stool and showed me how to do my job. I could hardly believe that all I had to do was to buckle sandal straps on uppers strung together in lots of a dozen pairs. Ada said it was done to prevent the sandal straps flapping about and getting in the way when soles were put on the uppers in the Cobbling Room.

Whilst I got on with the buckling, I surveyed my table companions. There were six teenage girls and three married women. The girls were making felt bows for trimming slippers. The women were placing templates over vamps (the toe section of the uppers) and marking each one at the exact spot where a machinist would attach the heel section.

I gazed across the room at the machinists seated six on each side of the many long tables. Above them were the shafting wheels, round which leather belts spun endlessly and powered the machines. I stared fascinated by it all until Ada turned to me and said, 'You'll have to get a move on, luv, or you'll never make a wage when you get on piece.'

My starting wage of nineteen shillings and ten pence per week (two pence less than £1) was paid on a fixed hourly rate that gave newcomers time to get used to the job before they were put on piece. Ada told me that, on piece, I would be paid three farthings a gross for buckling (four farthings made a penny). I said that was quite good for fastening 144 buckles. Ada laughed. 'A slipper mill gross is 144 pairs.' So three farthings didn't seem at all good for fastening 288 buckles.

The days seemed very long. Sitting in one place doing the same thing was so different from school, where a variety of lessons had made the time pass swiftly; here it dragged slowly, hour by boring hour. The only diversion came on Saturday morning when table-girls, who were not on piece work, had to clean the lavatories!

The best day of the week was Friday, when wages were paid. The whirring of sewing machines stopped as the women looked with eager anticipation at the clock on the wall. Promptly at eleven o'clock, the office girls appeared with the wage trays; they were made of wood and divided into honeycomb sections, each one containing an individual wage. When it was your turn you went to the desk and gave your number, then your wage with its payslip was scooped from the tray and put in your hand.

How proud and thrilled I was on the day I ran home with my first wage. Mother gave me half-a-crown (two shillings and six pence) for spending money. Margaret (who got six pence a week) was filled with envy and I preened with satisfaction. Well, there were times when I envied her absorption in grammar school life. She talked endlessly about school and it all sounded wonderful compared to my dreary days at the mill. So now I enjoyed being the one in an enviable situation.

In addition to my spending money, I was given four pence for Union dues, which were collected on payday. Ada had told me that if I didn't join the Union, nobody would work with me. I also needed three pence for a raffle ticket. Raffles were held weekly in aid of the mill's Comforts Fund for employees now serving in the armed forces. Dad said that I could give the three pence but I must not accept a raffle ticket because trying to get something for nothing was wrong. I said, 'Three pence isn't nothing.' But he insisted that raffles were a form of gambling, which was also wrong.

It was no use arguing with Dad when he got going about right and wrong, so that afternoon, when the woman selling raffle tickets came round, I gave her three pence and said that I didn't want the ticket. She stared at me. 'What's up wi' you? It's your bloody ticket.' She threw it on the table. The girls nudged each other and tittered. One of them said something I couldn't hear and they all laughed. I felt awful.

When I told Dad what had happened he quoted in his pulpit voice:

> Dare to be a Daniel,
> Dare to stand alone.
> Dare to have a purpose,
> Dare to make it known.'

I didn't want to stand alone and be laughed at, so never again did I refuse to accept a raffle ticket.

Wakes Week came in July. Almost everyone in the Girls' Room, including me, was going to Blackpool. Rita was sending black looks towards the machinists who were not concentrating on their work. Nobody was; the room was a-buzz with happy anticipation. After work stopped, everyone ran to the cloakroom where older women laughingly gave us young girls advice regarding our conduct in deliciously sinful Blackpool, with its wartime population of RAF lads. 'Keep yer hand on yer ha'penny,' they told us and added the assurance that, when we came back, they would look behind our ears 'to see if you've been up to owt yer shouldn't'.

None of this applied to me because I was too young to be interested in boys. All I wanted was to be in Blackpool, where I really belonged. I was warmly welcomed back into the family and had a wonderful time, especially when Uncle Lennie arrived for his annual holiday. It was like old times, with Uncle taking my cousins and me swimming and picnicking.

There was a new addition to our group. Uncle had brought with him a lady called Betty Hall. She had dark hair, lovely brown eyes and a gentle charm that instantly appealed to me, so, when Uncle told me that he and Betty were going to get married and that I would be able to stay with them for holidays, I was delighted.

The week ended all too soon; I was very sad when I had to go home and back to the mill, but soon after my return things changed. My boredom with buckling was somewhat relieved when Rita made me her errand girl. In those days there were no internal telephones, so I carried messages around the mill. This was interesting because it gave me the opportunity to see the entire manufacturing process. New recruits were not given a tour of the production line, so you could work for years in the room in which you had started and never see inside any of the others.

I sped happily up and down the mill, but being Rita's errand girl soon made me unpopular with the other table-girls. They called me 'Rita's pet' and accused me of having my sights set on 'a white coat' (becoming a boss). And they said I was 'stuck up' because I 'talked cut glass and lace curtains'. I didn't, but, as I had not grown up in Rossendale, my speech was different from theirs, which was flavoured with the local dialect. One day I got fed up with their jeers; I put on a la-di-da accent and said, 'Kindly stop boring me with stupid remarks.'

Reacting in a superior manner was the worst thing I could have done. Bella said, 'We'll get you after work and bring you down a peg or two with a good bashing.' I had never dreamed that they might retaliate with physical violence, so I was very frightened, especially of Bella who was a big intimidating girl. I knew that I didn't stand a chance if the girls attacked me on the way home because the older women would not be there to protect me. They worked until half past five, but young girls worked shorter hours so we left at five o'clock.

After Rita released us, I hung around for ten minutes to make sure that the girls had got fed up with waiting for me and gone home, then I went down to the mill yard. Nobody was there. Highly relieved I went along the road beside the river. Suddenly I heard feet pounding behind me. I looked back; the girls were in hot pursuit. Frantic with terror I scrambled up onto the wall flanking the riverbank. There was a long drop on the other side but I gripped my lip between my teeth and jumped. I landed with a jarring crash; my bent knees hit my chin and drove my top teeth into my lower lip. I stood up with blood streaming down my chin. The girls peered over the wall; when they saw the state I was in, they fled.

When I got home, Mother stared in disgust at my gashed lip. 'You're in a fine mess,' she said. And that was all. But when Dad came in from work he was very concerned. I didn't want to talk about what had happened at work, so I just muttered that I'd fallen over a kerb.

The next morning when I arrived at work with a gaping swollen lip, the women gasped in horror. 'Who did that?' Ada demanded. She looked hard at the girls who were keeping their heads down to their work. Just then Rita came to our table. She stared at my face. 'Betty! What on earth's happened to you?' I glanced at the girls; they looked very apprehensive. They were certainly going to cop it from Rita if I told how they they'd threatened to beat me up and chased me. But I didn't tell. I knew that it wasn't all down to them, so I said that I'd fallen down our cellar steps.

We all settled down to work. A few minutes later a bag of caramels appeared under my nose and Bella said, ''Ere, 'ave a toffee.' I knew it was a peace offering, so I took one and said, 'Ta very much' instead of thank you. I had learned my lesson; it didn't do to be different, so from then on I copied the way in which my workmates talked and there was no more trouble.

All the same, as the months went by I became increasingly fed up with the mill and desperate to get away. It wouldn't have been so bad if I'd had the challenge of earning more money on piecework, but this hadn't happened because I was still running errands for Rita. 'She's making a mug of you,' Ada told me. 'It's high time you were promoted to a sewing machine.' Some of the other table girls were now on machines, but the prospect of this step-up in the room's hierarchy gave me no joy.

Strange feelings had started coming over me. Suddenly, a terrible desolation would well up inside me and the tears would start. One day, as I sat buckling sandals, I looked across the room at the rows of women bent over the machines, their plump bottoms spreading over the stools on which they sat for hours every day. As I stared at those rows of bottoms I suddenly thought, *Is that what I shall become... a fat bottom on a stool? Is that all there is for me for the rest of my life?* Panic rose and flared through me. I fled to the cloakroom and wept bitterly in a locked lavatory.

But it couldn't all have been down to my unhappiness at work. I was now fifteen; I had at last started to develop a bust and a slim waist, so probably havoc caused by hormones was partly responsible for my emotional distress. But I didn't know about hormones, or that strange feelings were a part of growing up.

However, a new work prospect unexpectedly arose. On my way home from the mill I met Mrs Evans. She said, 'You look fed up, luv, what's up?' I told her that I hated the mill and wanted to leave. She said that she could speak for me at The Mount, a mill owner's mansion where she worked as a cleaner. Their maids had been called up to work on munitions, so girls too young for call-up were required. 'You'd have to live in,' Mrs Evans said, 'but they are nice people to work for and you'd get plenty of time off. I'm sure they'll take you on when I say what a good worker you are at home.'

Any job was better than the mill, so I ran home full of glee and told Mother that I was probably going to be a maid at The Mount. 'You'll do no such thing,' she said firmly. 'You'd be nothing but a skivvy on a live-in wage of five shillings a week!'

'And if I go you'll lose your skivvy and my wage,' I said sarcastically. 'Well, I'm fed up with being your drudge, so I'm going and you can't stop me.'

'You will do as you are told,' she exploded.

I saw red. 'Oh no I won't. You are not my mother so you can't tell me what to do!' She stared at me stunned. Oh, crikey! I'd let it out – the thing I wasn't supposed to know. I turned and ran up to the attic, where I sat on my bed and waited fearfully for Dad to come home. I knew that Mother would tell him what had happened.

I heard the front door open. A few minutes later Dad

came up to the attic. 'Who told you?' he said quietly. Despite all the time that had passed since my discovery of the secret, I couldn't admit the truth; I still felt guilty about my nosy snooping and said that one of my cousins had told me.

He said, 'I was going to tell you when you were twenty-one.' Then he sat down beside me. 'I met your mother, courted, married and lost her all within two years. I was heartbroken when she died. We'd been so happy and we never had a wrong word.' I wanted to ask why she had died, but grief for Dad's loss, and mine, overwhelmed and choked me, so I couldn't get a word out. Then he told me, 'When the mother you have now took you on, she knew nothing about babies, but she looked after you, changed your nappies, did everything for you. I was so grateful to her, and I still am.'

But I didn't want to hear about her. 'My mother,' I said huskily, 'what—?'

'She was called Emily. She had lovely wavy hair and beautiful eyes. I'll show you her photo.' I wanted to know more, but I was struggling to hold back a rising flood of tears. I couldn't speak; the dam would have burst. Dad, too, seemed to be stuck for words. Suddenly, he stood up and said, 'Look, I do know that things haven't been easy for you. You haven't always had your crack of the whip, but you'll always be all right while I'm here.' Then he went downstairs and the tears I'd been holding back burst forth.

The next morning I overslept, so, although I ran all the way, I was late for work. Eight o'clock was starting time; at three minutes past, the mill door was shut and locked. Latecomers were penalised by loss of money that could have been earned during the time spent standing outside until the door was unlocked at half-past-eight.

I stood leaning against the mill wall along with a few other people who'd been locked out. The woman standing next to me was very distressed. She said she was late because she'd had to go and find someone to look after her daughter, who was too poorly to be sent to school. I thought it very unfair for her be locked out when she had a very good reason for being late.

At half-past-eight the mill owner, Mr Holt, emerged from the office and came across the mill yard to where we stood. He didn't speak to us, but he never gave anyone, except Rita, so much as a nod when he stalked through our room on his daily tour of the mill. So now he walked slowly along our line with his hands clasped behind his back and gave each of us a cold, contemptuous stare. I was amazed! Wasn't loss of pay sufficient penalty for being late, without this shaming performance? Then, having humiliated and intimidated everyone to his satisfaction, he unlocked the door and let us in.

I felt humiliated, but intimidated I was not. I stamped up the steps, blazing with fury. I was not going to stay here and be treated like dirt. I was going to find another job and to hell with Mother. I was ready to walk out there and then if Rita had started on me for being late; but when I sat down at the table she only gave me a black look.

At home I preserved a sullen silence. Probably, in view of what Dad had told me about my stepmother's care for me when I was a baby, he expected my attitude towards her to change. It didn't. I was not grateful for something I couldn't remember; I only knew the way things were now.

I waited for Dad to show me my real mother's photo, but he must have forgotten his intention. Still, I longed to know what she had looked like, so, one day when everyone was out of the house, I searched Dad's desk drawers. I found a studio portrait of a young lady; and as I gazed at her cloud of wavy hair and her beautiful eyes, I knew that I was looking at my mother. I stole the photograph. Dad never missed it; or if he did he never said anything to me. I waited in vain for him to tell me more about my mother, but her picture became a great comfort to me; I looked at it when I felt lonely and bereft.

But, before long, loneliness and sadness came to an end; my life changed for the better.

Chapter 12

Someone told me that assistants were required by Woolworths. I smartened myself up and got an interview with the manageress, Miss Farley. She said that I could join the staff as soon as I had worked out my notice at the mill. I was jubilant. I knew that Mother wouldn't object, nor did she because the wage was three shillings more than I was paid at the mill.

I loved working at Woolworths. It was a small store with a dozen counters. I was in charge of the hardware counter and I kept it like a new pin. I even polished the padlocks on display and dusted the piles of loose nails with a paintbrush.

Many of the original staff had been called up, which was why girls like me who were below call-up age were being taken on. Miss Farley, who was middle-aged, had replaced the male manager who'd also been called up.

She was strict; she had to be to cope with a bunch of giddy fifteen-year-olds. But she was very fond of her girls. She used to say that after we had all gone home she felt as if she'd put a family to bed. Indeed she created a real family atmosphere in our store. She always concluded staff training sessions by reminding us that she was there for us if we needed help or advice about anything, whatever it might be.

She was always on the lookout for ways in which she could help her staff. One day, after she'd overheard two of us trying to think up ways of earning money for a holiday, she offered to pay each of us half-a-crown every Saturday for sweeping the floor twice daily and stoking the boiler.

Normally all the staff took their turn at floor sweeping and Miss Farley herself stoked the boiler in the cellar, from where she emerged breathless and dusty. It took thirty shovels of coke to fill the boiler.

She did not add the half-crown to our wages; it was given to us separately, so Mother knew nothing about it and I didn't tell her because she would have claimed it. I hadn't forgotten how she had kept the whole of my Wakes Week holiday pay from the mill. It was the custom for mill girls to be allowed to keep their holiday pay for boarding house accommodation and spending money. I'd stayed with Auntie Jessie, so I didn't need digs money; but I was not given any spending money from my holiday pay, so I had gone almost penniless to Blackpool.

One of the best things about working in Woolworths was the lively new friends I gained. We had a great time. On Tuesday afternoons, when the store was closed, we went swimming at Haslingden Baths, or to tea dances at Bury Palais. And in the evenings we all went to the Rawtenstall youth club, where we played table tennis and danced to records of the popular swing bands played on a radiogram. But Dad, determined to keep me unspotted by the world, had started checking up on me. He disapproved of my association with the Woolworths girls; he wanted to pin me down to Sunday school activities; but I'd had enough of a set up where there were hymns and prayers with everything.

Probably Dad's anxiety was due to the fact that I had at last started my periods, which, as Mother had told me, meant that I could now have a baby. At that time, this didn't seem to have anything to do with me, so I hardly gave it a thought, but in Dad's view I was now at risk. I got thoroughly exasperated by his constant queries about where I had been and who I had been with, so I rebelled and did things specifically forbidden, such as going with my friends on the Rabbit Run. This was on Sunday evenings when, as the youth club and the cinemas were closed, there was nothing to do. So the town's teenagers promenaded back and forth along Bank Street, the girls linking arms in twos and the boys ambling in groups. On winter nights, when it was pitch-dark because of the blackout, couples necking in shop doorways were flushed out by a policeman's torch. We were always supervised by authority on our endless trekking back and forth.

Another forbidden activity was going to the Astoria ballroom. All my friends went, so I didn't see why I should not be allowed to go. But Dad said that it was no place for young girls because it was frequented by drinkers from the pub nearby. We girls never saw any drinkers; we just enjoyed dancing with each other or boys from the youth club to a very good band; and that was all we did. So I continued to disobey Dad.

One Saturday night at the Astoria, I was standing talking to friends when suddenly, to my horror, I saw Dad surveying the scene from the arched entrance to the ballroom. I hastily ducked down behind the crowd lining the dance floor and crept to the cloakroom. When I got back, Dad had gone. I breathed a sigh of relief. I didn't think he'd seen me but, in view of what happened soon after, I was wrong.

A few weeks earlier my family had left Omerod Street for a modern semi on Park Avenue. Before we moved in, Mother had sent me to scrub all the floors. She said that the former tenants had been Catholics, so she wasn't moving in until it had all been thoroughly scrubbed. This was absurd, but I wasn't surprised because it was typical of her religious bigotry, which included the view that all Catholics were ignorant and kept mucky houses. It made no sense to me; several of my friends were Catholics, but neither I nor they cared a jot about our different religious connections, nor did they live in mucky houses.

We had only been in the house for a few weeks when Mother happened to go downstairs during the night and found the kitchen floor black with cockroaches. She was furious and disgusted. 'Well!' she fumed. 'What else can you expect from Catholics.' She said that she would look for another house straight away. I laughed and said that she'd better find a Catholic-free house because I wasn't going to do any more scrubbing. But I didn't laugh when I discovered how badly a house move was going to affect me.

The following week, Miss Farley called me into her office. I had spent some time that morning checking the hardware shelves in the stock room, so I thought that, as was usual, she wanted to see my list of goods needing to be reordered.

I got a shock when she said, 'Your father has been in; he said that you have to leave and he gave me your notice.'

I stared at her, stunned. 'But… why?'

'He said you are moving to Newchurch and that it's too far away for you to continue working here.'

'But I could easily come on the bus,' I cried. (Newchurch was only two miles distant from Rawtenstall's Woolworths.)

'That's what I said,' Miss Farley nodded. 'But moving house isn't the only reason why you have to leave. Your father feels that the girls here are a bad influence on you.' She eyed me closely. 'Now, you had better tell me what you have all been up to.' Then it dawned on me: Dad had seen me at the Astoria.

I could see that Miss Farley was very annoyed by Dad's accusation that her girls were a bad influence, so I told her that we had only been going to dances at the Astoria. (I thought it best not to let on about the Rabbit Run.)

Her eyebrows shot up in surprise. 'Dancing! Is that all?' I assured her that it was. 'Well!' she said. And the amazed, what's wrong with that, way she said it told me that she was on my side. She'd certainly done her best for me. She said,

'I told your father that you are a credit to the store and I don't want to lose you, but I'm afraid it was no use.'

When I got home I raised the roof but that was no use, either. Dad said that he already had another job lined up for me, near to the new house.

We moved into an enormous house known as 'The Old Parsonage', in the hilltop village of Newchurch. I can't remember the date carved above the door, but the house was very old. There was a sundial above the date stone, and there was a pigeon loft in the roof pediment. On the front of the house were ten windows; fortunately they all had interior wooden shutters, so they didn't need blackout curtains. Downstairs were dining and sitting rooms, plus a study, all with polished oak floors. There were stone slab floors in the kitchen, the larder and a huge scullery/washhouse. An impressive carved oak staircase led up to five bedrooms and a bathroom with a lavatory. An ordinary flight of stairs went up to four attics. There were cellars, outhouses and a front lawn with a greengage tree.

We certainly did not need such a large house and the rent must have been high. But Mother was delighted with her prestige residence. I wasn't. I knew who was going to have to clean it.

A few days after we moved in, I found myself back in a slipper mill. The road running through the valley bottom was lined with mills and not much else, so only mill work was to be had. I was seething with fury that Monday morning, as I went down steep Turnpike to the Irwell Mill.

My new job was in the Press Room, where boot and shoe soles were cut by sole-shaped knives from sheets of leather spread beneath automatic presses. The foreman, Alf, greeted me with, "Ello, luv. I know yer daddy.' I immediately assumed that Alf was a church member and thus deemed, by Dad, suitable to be in charge of me. But he turned out to be one of Dad's insurance clients.

Alf took me to a table where a man called Norman was stacking soles in tall wooden bins with narrow slots. Opposite the bins, two girls were putting soles into size-grading machines. My job was to pick up the soles and carry them to Norman's table.

I wandered back and forth with piles of soles, but for most of the time I had nothing to do because the graders did not produce enough soles to keep me going. I soon got fed up with hanging about. I had thought that nothing could be more boring than sandal buckling, but this was far worse.

When I got home at dinnertime I told Dad that I hated my new job because I had next to nothing to do. But he only joked, 'Count the bricks in the wall!'

'I've already done that,' I said bitterly, as he beat a quick retreat through the door on his way to work.

Back at the mill I asked Norman why he couldn't do the sole transfers himself – his table was only a few steps away from the graders. He said that he had a painful back condition that prevented him from carrying anything. But no doubt he feared to lose my help if Alf realised that I was doing nothing for most of the time. He told me that when there were no soles awaiting transfer I must 'go for a walk'. So I wandered off to the toilets where I met two girls, who remembered seeing me at the Astoria.

Alice and Margie were very friendly. 'Come and 'ave a fag,' Alice said. We sat on the floor in one of the cubicles and I smoked my first cigarette. The cubicle was very small, so we were rather cramped. We had to avoid leaning our backs against the whitewashed brick walls because they were adorned with disgusting brown splotches. Some lines were scrawled on the wall:

> When you come into this hall,
> Use the paper, not the wall.
> For it is a dirty trick
> To wipe your bottom on a brick.'

There was never any toilet paper so most people, apart from the finger-users, provided their own. Nor was there anywhere to wash your hands.

Alice and Margie worked in the warehouse, where there must have been a lag in the production line because they often went for a walk. They soon introduced me to enjoyable ways of beguiling the time and, as we were not on piecework, our wages were unaffected by our absences.

We were always hungry, so we often nipped out of a side door and went across the road to a chip shop where we feasted on three-penny mixtures (chips and mushy peas). Or we went to Margie's house on a street behind the mill, where we had tea and toast. Her parents were out at work, so there was nobody to question our illicit presence. We couldn't go to Alice's house because her mother was at home looking after Alice's little sister, Lucy, who was very ill with tuberculosis. The disease was rife; it killed 25,000 people a year in the UK. I remember a young woman called Marie who worked in the Press Room. She was as thin as a rake and she looked quite scary with her glittering eyes and scarlet-flushed cheeks set in a sunken face that curved like a crescent moon from forehead to chin. Poor Marie worked until not long before she died. She was only thirty-seven. On the day of her funeral, I carried the Press Room's wreath to her house.

The following week, Alice came to work in tears: little Lucy had died. A few days after the funeral, Alice asked Margie and me to go with her to consult a man who was a spiritualist. She said, 'I want to ask him if our Lucy is all right.' I wasn't keen to go, especially when Alice said that the man would tell our fortunes for a shilling. I thought that he was probably a fraud – like La Celeste on the Blackpool Pleasure Beach; but I couldn't resist a jaunt away from the mill, so, in the end, I agreed to go.

We sneaked out of the mill and went to a cellar dwelling beneath a terrace of decrepit houses beside the river. Alice knocked on a door and we went in.

It was a small stone-floored cellar that reeked of cabbage, damp and dirt. It was sparsely furnished with a battered old table and a backless kitchen chair. There was an ancient fire oven-range and the grate was full of rubbish. I had never seen such squalor.

The door to the kitchen opened and a wizened looking man came in. He had stubbly ginger hair and ferrety eyes. His flannel shirt was filthy and he stank of stale sweat. He said, ''Ello, girls.' Then he looked at me and said, 'I've not seen you before.' I thought that he was certainly not going to see me again. But, for now, I had to go along with Alice and Margie, so, when it was my turn, I went into the smelly kitchen to have my fortune told.

I sat on a chair; beside me, a single rusty tap dripped onto a slimy slopstone piled with dirty pots. The man sat opposite with his knees almost touching mine. He tried to draw me out with questions obviously designed to elicit information on which he could base his so-called fortune telling. But I refused to be drawn.

Then he got hold of my hand; I snatched it back. 'Now then,' he grinned, 'don't get yer 'air off; I'm only going to read yer palm. Yer want yer bob's worth, don't yer?'

I can't remember what he said; I just wanted to get away from that horrible man and his awful den. I flung my shilling down and escaped.

On our walk back to the mill, Margie happily described the golden future awaiting her; it was exactly what she'd wanted to hear – a tall dark, handsome man and a happy marriage. Alice was solemnly awed. She said, 'He brought our Lucy back to me and she's all right.' I thought it had been a ridiculous waste of my shilling, but I didn't say a word because Alice and Margie felt that they had got their bobs' worth.

I also went along with another activity that passed the time when we had no work to do. We would go into a small rest room, where Alice set out her version of an Ouija board. The letters of the alphabet were placed in a circle on the floor with a glass tumbler in the centre. We knelt down with each of us resting a finger on the glass, which obligingly answered questions by sliding to and fro and pointing to the letters Y-E-S or N-O. Queries were mostly of a hopeful nature concerning boys: 'Will Jack take me home after the dance on Saturday?', 'Will Les ask me out again?' and so forth. The answer was almost always, Y-E-S so I thought that we must somehow be pushing the glass.

Before long, other girls heard about the Ouija board and came to join us. A girl called Sadie asked the glass, 'Will I have to get married?' So we all knew what she'd been up to. Every eye was riveted on the glass as it slid towards the letter N. Then it changed direction, homed in on the letter Y and stopped. Sadie howled, 'Make yer bloody mind up!' and we all burst out laughing.

Suddenly the door flew open and there stood Alf. 'Right, you lot,' he yelled, 'get back to work!'

A few days later, a young lad who worked on a skiver was called up. I was taken off sole-carrying and put on the skiver. Small pieces of stiff board called 'bits' were skived (thinned) along one edge by passing them between a revolving, bowl-shaped knife and a metal plate.

I didn't know what the bits were for, nor did I care. It was boring, appallingly repetitive work for which I was paid the piece-rate of two pence per gross. Although I was doing the same job as the lad who'd been called up, my pay was less than his because I was a girl. I was really fed up; I could no longer skive off work for hours with Margie and Alice; they'd gone to work on munitions. Anyway I had to keep at it to take home a wage at least equal to the time rate I'd been paid for sole-carrying, or I would certainly have had my spending money promptly reduced by Mother.

The skiver was mounted on a tall iron post; it was too high for me, so Alf brought a board for me to stand on, but it made little difference. I had to lift my right shoulder and tilt my elbow at an awkward angle to get my hand on a level with the plate and the knife. This distorted posture made my shoulder ache; but it was just something else to be put up with.

Furthermore, I had to spend several evenings a week scrubbing stone floors and cleaning bedrooms etc. in the Parsonage. But, when I was let out, I caught a bus to the youth club where I thoroughly enjoyed being with my friends. Before long, I fell in love.

Each of my girlfriends fancied a boy and talked endlessly about him. I didn't want to be left out, so when I was told that Danny Taylor fancied me, although I couldn't think why he should, I promptly fell in love with him.

Danny didn't play table tennis or dance; he never walked me home, nor, as far as I can remember, did we speak to each other. But that didn't matter. Being in love at a distance was satisfyingly thrilling. It was tremendously exciting just to see Danny and sightings were recorded in my diary. I recall one entry: 'I shall remember this day for the rest of my life!'

It was my seventh-heaven reaction to a brief encounter with Danny in the village chip shop where he had smiled at me, a brilliant blue-eyed smile that had made my heart turn over. Well, I have remembered it for the rest of my life; and now the memory of that exhilarating delight in romantic fancy takes me back to my springtime, when life and love were new.

Perhaps this all seems very tame to my grandchildren's generation, but, for mine, it was a wonderful part of growing up.

Chapter 13

Dancing was another bright star in my sky, so, when our youth club members were invited to a Friday evening dance at Haslingden's youth club, I very much wanted to go. But on Fridays I was always kept in to scrub stone floors in the Parsonage, so I knew that I hadn't a hope of going to the dance.

When Friday came, fate took a hand. I got home from work to find that Auntie Maggie had arrived from Nelson. No doubt Mother didn't want me around, turning the wireless volume up at full blast and singing at the top of my voice when she and Auntie wanted to talk – I always expressed my defiant fury at being kept in as noisily as I could to annoy Mother – so she let me go to the dance.

It was held in the spacious hall of Haslingden's junior school; the Blue Bandits had been hired to play, so it was rather superior to our youth club's hops with records played on a radiogram.

It was a very warm evening, so, after a hectic jitterbugging session, I went to cool off on one of the benches lining the walls. A boy moved along to make room for me and I sat down beside him. He asked if I was enjoying the dance. I said, 'Yes. It's smashing.' He told me that he had organised the dance and that he was the youth club's president.

Suddenly I remembered that I'd seen him before. One night, a Haslingden youth club team had come to our club for a 'Brains Trust' contest. This title came from a popular wireless programme in which opposing teams answered questions – it was the forerunner of the 'quiz.' I had been in our team (brains were not essential) and on the Haslingden side there had been a tall, dark boy who I thought was a right know-all.

At the conclusion of the contest (know-all's team won), he started a discussion about something. I was very irritated: some of us were waiting to play a table tennis match, but we couldn't put the tables up whilst he was holding forth. I wished he'd shut up and buzz off.

But, on the night of the dance, I was far from annoyed by the know-all. In fact my reaction to him was very different. I was completely fascinated by his sparkling vivacity. As we talked, it seemed to me that he inhabited a world entirely different from mine. He told me that he was studying for a chemistry degree at Blackburn Technical College. I didn't tell him what I did. He asked my name and gave me a small printed card; it said: 'Ted Barnes, Magician. Terms on application.' I was very impressed. Never had I met a boy with so many interests and such lively enthusiasm.

At half past nine I reluctantly said, 'I have to go now.' I had to get a bus to Rawtenstall in time to catch the last bus to Newchurch, which left at ten o'clock. Bus services finished early during the War. Ted escorted me to the bus stop. We stood chatting, then, when the bus appeared in the distance, he said, 'Are you doing anything tomorrow night?' I pretended to consider this, then I said casually, 'No, I don't think I've got anything on.' Of course I hadn't.

'Will you go with me to the cinema?' he asked. The bus was drawing to a halt; I said yes and we hastily arranged to meet at half past seven outside Rawtenstall's library, then the bus carried me away. I rode home on cloud nine.

I spent Saturday morning and afternoon in thrilled anticipation of my first date. When I got to the library, Ted was waiting. He'd booked seats in the circle at the Pavilion Cinema. When we were settled, he proffered Markovitch cigarettes in a smart black and white striped box with a man in a top hat on the lid. I had never seen such classy cigarettes and if Ted was trying to impress me, he certainly succeeded.

The film was Noel Coward's *In Which We Serve*. It was about the Royal Navy's war at sea. I had never taken much interest in the War; it hadn't really affected me. I was just living the intensely self-absorbed life of a teenager. But as I watched the young sailors dying in torpedoed ships, realisation suddenly struck me: the vibrantly alive boy sitting next to me could be called up and killed! I was filled with terror for him. During the interval I asked him if he would have to join up. He said that his war service had been deferred until the completion of his college course. But that didn't put my mind at rest; who knew for how long the War was going to last.

When we left the cinema, we had to run for my bus. On Saturdays there was a late bus to Newchurch that I had to catch; Dad was very strict about me getting home by eleven o'clock. The bus was just pulling away, so I only had time to hastily thank Ted as I leapt aboard.

I arrived home completely deflated; Ted hadn't asked to see me again. I told myself that he hadn't had the chance to ask because we'd had to dash for my bus. But, on the other hand, I thought it unlikely that a boy as clever as Ted could really be interested in ordinary me.

The following evening I joined my friends on the Rabbit Run. It was a beautiful autumn evening and still broad daylight because of Double British Summertime. The clocks had gone forward two hours instead of the customary one; this measure had been introduced by the Government to allow extra production time on the land. Growing food to feed the nation was a priority because importing food would have put the lives of sailors at risk, and diverted ships from fighting the war at sea.

We strolled to and fro. Normally, I would have been keeping an eye open for Danny, but overnight I'd lost all interest in him.

Suddenly, I was conscious of someone close behind me. I glanced round; much to my surprise and delight it was Ted. He walked with me to Newchurch, where we sat in the mini-park opposite the Parsonage and talked. He asked me where I worked. I didn't want to admit that I was a mill girl, but I had no option. I told him that I worked at the Irwell Mill. But my fear that this would demean me in Ted's eyes and cause him to lose interest in me was immediately relieved. He only nodded and asked me to go with him to a variety theatre in Blackburn the following Saturday. Then, when we heard the bus grinding up the steep Turnpike, I said, 'You'd better go or you'll have a long walk home.' It was six miles from Newchurch to Haslingden, the hilltop town at the other end of the valley where Ted lived. I saw him to the bus stop and then I went home, on top of the world again.

When Saturday came we went by bus to Blackburn. We spent the afternoon rowing on Queen's Park Lake, then, after we'd had our tea in a chip shop café, we went to the theatre. It was all a new experience for me, especially the exciting thrill of anticipation when the orchestra in the pit burst forth with a lively tune and the stage footlights lit up the curtains. The entertainers included a comedian, performing dogs, acrobats, jugglers and the star of the show, a pianist and singer called Turner Layton who sang, 'When You're Smiling (The Whole World Smiles with You)'. It certainly seemed as if the world was smiling with me on that happy day.

Our subsequent dates were on an irregular basis. During the week Ted was busy with his college work; and on Saturdays he was often booked to do a magic show at Sunday school concerts. In addition he was in the 'All

Aboard' concert party; the members gave their services free in aid of the forces' comforts funds, so they were in great demand.

Furthermore, as Ted had not been called up, he had to serve in the Home Guard and take part in Sunday operations up on the hills, where they practised repelling German invaders played by members of an army platoon.

On one such occasion Ted got into trouble. His Home Guard platoon had been ordered to disable a 'German' tank. When it appeared over the brow of a hill, they ordered the crew out at rifle point, which stopped the tank's progress; but it was not disabled, so Ted levered off its caterpillar tracks. The army took a very dim view of Ted's marooning of its tank on the hills. Complaints ensued; but the Home Guard's captain only laughed and complimented Ted for showing initiative and 'getting one up on the army'.

Dad wasn't at all happy about me going out with a boy about whom he knew nothing. He told me, 'If you want a boyfriend, get one from the Sunday school.' He naively thought that anyone connected with the Church must be respectable and trustworthy, i.e. no sex before marriage.

He expected me to follow the customary mode of Baptist church courtship, which began when a boy asked a girl to go for a Sunday walk. Eventually, after walks and cinema visits, the girl was invited to tea at the boy's house, where the best tablecloth and a china tea service would be brought out for the occasion. Subsequently he was invited to tea at the girl's house; it was then accepted by everyone that marriage would follow in due course.

One Sunday evening I had a heavy cold, so Dad said that I was not to go out. I told him, 'I have to go because Ted will be waiting for me at the library.' Dad promptly seized that as his chance to check up on Ted. He sent Margaret to the library; she was to tell Ted that I had to stay in the house because I had a cold, but he was welcome to come back with her.

They duly appeared and I introduced Ted to my family. Before long, much to my embarrassment, Dad started interrogating Ted.

'Do you drink?' he demanded sternly. Ted said he didn't. I should have known that drinking would be Dad's first concern. His father had been an alcoholic; this had resulted in a great deal of family suffering, so Dad had frequently told me, 'Never, never marry a man who drinks.'

The next important question was, 'Do you go to church?' Ted said he did, so he passed muster. They continued to talk. I can't remember the subjects they discussed, but Ted easily kept his end up until it was time for his bus. I saw him to the front door. Outside he said 'Phew!' and did a mock collapse of relief.

We said goodnight and I went back to hear Dad's verdict. He didn't say a word, so, as no objections were made, I assumed that Ted was accepted as a suitable boyfriend for me.

But Mother thought he was too good for me. After Dad had gone upstairs, she said, 'I don't know what an intelligent boy like him can see in you.' I didn't either, so her sneer didn't do a lot for my confidence.

The following spring we moved out of the Parsonage. The village drapery was for sale. Mother had once worked in a draper's shop, so she'd had some experience of the trade. She borrowed some money from Uncle Arthur and bought the stock and good will. By then the debt to Uncle Lennie must have been paid off.

We all crammed into the terrace property between the pub and the post office. The shop took up the front room; behind it was a very small living room. There was a kitchen with room only for an oven and a sink. Steps led down to a coal cellar. And, oh joy! We'd got another backyard petty. Upstairs were three bedrooms, one of which had a bath but no washbasin. On a stool there was a bowl to be filled from the bath taps. I slept in a bed beside the bath. The window didn't open, so the room was damp and steamy when I retired on bath nights. But the hot water tank kept the room warm in winter.

For me, the best thing about the move was the reduction in house cleaning. The worst was Mother's insistence that I must wear some of the old stock that emerged from the deep drawers beneath the counter. There were two linen dresses: one was shocking pink, the other a gooseberry green. And there was a dreary brown dress with horrible squiggles crawling all over it. All were in styles from the year dot. I protested, but Mother pointed out the good quality of the materials and said that I should be grateful. I was not.

Then she presented me with a pair of thick schoolgirl knickers, but they were not the customary navy blue that I wouldn't have minded; they were bright red! I was horrified. 'I'm not going to wear those!' But Mother said that it didn't matter what colour my knickers were because 'nobody would see what I had on underneath'. She was wrong about that.

One day, when I was wearing the knickers, I went on a youth club ramble over the hills. We came to a stile; I climbed up and jumped down on the other side. Well, *I* jumped but my skirt didn't; it was caught up on a sliver of wood. So there I was hooked up, and coming along the path behind me half-a-dozen lads were getting an eyeful of my appalling red knickers. Frantically I tugged and wrenched, then one of the boys ran to my aid and freed my skirt. My face must have been as red as my knickers. When I got home I buried them in the dustbin.

But that wasn't the end of my embarrassment. An

account of our ramble appeared in the youth club's monthly magazine. Reference was made to 'an interesting and colourful new style of rambling apparel worn by one of the girls'.

The magazine's editor, Bill, was always on the look out for material, so when he asked me to write something for the next edition I obliged with a feature called 'Removals'. As Mother was a serial-mover, I considered myself to be an expert on the subject. My account of the chaos and upheaval involved in moving house duly appeared in the magazine and was followed by more articles. Then, when Bill was called up, I became the magazine's editor. I also sent reports of club activities to the local newspaper, the *Free Press*.

I also began trying to write poems. They were mostly filled with teenage self-dramatisation, but they provided release from steaming frustration; especially on summer mornings when the prospect of yet another day spent in the confines of the gloomy, noisy mill became unbearable. Then I got up very early and went up onto a hill behind the village, where I sat scribbling lines in which I hurled fury and defiance at the mill chimneys in the valley below and yearned for freedom, until the calm peace and beauty of the valley in the early morning sunshine stole over my senses and stilled my tumult. When smoke, fouling the clear air, began to rise from the mill chimneys, I went down the hill restored in spirit.

Not all of my poetic efforts were filled with sturm and drang. One evening, when Margaret was struggling to write a poem for her homework assignment, I helped her out with a simple poem called 'The Cat'.

Several weeks later, when Mother was entertaining some church friends to supper, she passed round Margaret's grammar school magazine and proudly said, 'See what Margaret has written.' I looked over a shoulder and saw

'The Cat' by Margaret Gibson. I laughed and said that I'd written it. 'You!' Mother scoffed. 'You couldn't have written that.'

'Well,' I said, 'ask Margaret who wrote it.' As it happened, Margaret was staying the night with a school friend. She was back the next day when I got home from work. Mother was tight-lipped and Margaret looked sheepish. Neither of them said a word to me, but I knew that the true author of 'The Cat' had been revealed. I couldn't help laughing to myself.

Chapter 14

It was at about this time that Dad at last told me more about Emily, my real mother. One evening, when we were alone in the house, he drew my attention to something I hadn't noticed: it was a small varicose vein in the calf of my left leg. He told me, 'Your mother had varicose veins in the same leg; she had poor circulation, like you.' I'd always had purplish hands and feet. In later years I learned that this is an inherited condition called 'Raynauds'. Prolonged standing can result in varicose veins, so no doubt the months I'd spent standing at the skiver had caused my vein to appear. But Emily's problem had been far more serious.

It was a sad story Dad told me that night. He had met Emily when he lived at Blackpool. She worked on an indoor market stall, where she had sold stockings. Standing all day had caused her varicosed leg to swell badly with phlebitis. During their courtship, Dad had taken her in a wheelchair for outings along the Promenade.

'When she recovered we got married,' he said. 'But we didn't have long together. She died suddenly, ten days after you were born. It was a terrible shock; I had no idea that anything was wrong.'

But, as Dad went on to tell me, it had transpired that a great deal had been wrong.

During her confinement, the varicose veins in Emily's leg caused something known as 'white leg'. This resulted in a blood clot that had travelled to her heart and killed her instantly. Then Dad discovered that Emily's two sisters, who'd looked after her during her confinement, had not given her the medicine prescribed by the doctor. Dad and Emily were Baptists, but the sisters were Christian Scientists; they believed in 'spiritual healing' so they never resorted to medicine. Dad accused the sisters of causing Emily's death and a tremendous row ensued.

Furthermore, Emily's death certificate stated that she had died from 'Aortic Stenosis and incompetence'. At the time Dad didn't know that 'incompetence' was a medical term that had nothing to do with Emily's nursing; he thought that it confirmed the sisters' neglect in failing to give Emily her medicine. But it is unlikely that the medicine available in those days could have saved Emily from deep vein thrombosis, especially as she'd had a defective heart valve.

I was deeply affected by what Dad had told me. That night I wasn't seeing him as just my dad; I was seeing him as a young man, bereft of his wife and left with a baby. I said, 'It must have been a dreadful time for you.'

But I was delighted to hear that I had aunties; I couldn't wait to find them. 'Where are they now?'

'I think they died years ago,' Dad said. 'Anyway, after I remarried and left Blackpool all contact was lost.' I was very disappointed. But thinking it over later, it seemed to me that there was something very odd about it all. Why had all contact between Dad and Emily's sisters been lost? Had the row between them after Emily's death permanently damaged their relationship? Had the sisters kept their distance because they felt some degree of guilt for Emily's death? Even so, how could they have entirely rejected their dead sister's child?

Many years later I learned that secrecy might have played its part in the rift. One day I asked Mother why, during my childhood, I had not been told that she was my stepmother. She said, 'Well, when your dad and I had our children we wanted you to be all alike. We didn't want you to feel any difference so we decided not to tell you until you had grown up.' I have no doubt that their decision was made in good faith and that Mother had truly intended to treat me as her own child. It hadn't worked out that way at all, but I didn't say so. By then there was no point in dragging up old conflict, to which I had contributed my share; nor did I feel that I could have done well in the difficult role of a stepmother.

However, the early decision to keep me in ignorance may have prevented any move on Dad's part to re-establish contact with Emily's sisters.

Of course this is surmise; Dad never told me any more about what had happened, but, whatever it was, I wish with all my heart that I could have known my mother's people.

One day a letter came from Uncle Lennie. He said that he and Betty Hall had got married and set up home in Worcester, so I must go and stay with them for a holiday.

When Wakes Week arrived, I went by train to Worcester. Uncle met me at the station and drove me to the house on Shrubbery Avenue, where Betty gave me a very warm welcome.

Uncle was almost bursting with pride as he showed me round the spacious Victorian house; he had lived in guesthouses for years, so he was revelling in his first real home. I was very impressed by the elegantly furnished rooms, especially my bedroom with its moss-green fitted carpet and gold curtains with a matching bedspread. Uncle was forty-two when he married, so, with the money saved during his bachelor years, he could afford to splash out on the house.

Betty was probably about the same age as Uncle. She was the manageress of a small hat shop near the cathedral. When Uncle was working, she took me with her to the shop where I helped to sell hats, which I greatly enjoyed because I was so happy just being with Betty. As the days went by, I basked in her warm, gentle friendship.

Uncle was a sales representative for the local gas board. When his work took him to outlying villages he took me along, and I enjoyed seeing the beautiful sunlit countryside. He taught me to row on the River Severn and I picnicked with him and Betty on the Malvern Hills. One evening Uncle took me to Evensong in the cathedral. I was held in thrall by it all; the stone columns soaring up to the magnificent roof, the swelling organ music, the ethereal singing of the choir and the golden glow of candles along the choir stalls.

In the evenings, from my bedroom window, I gazed down on the flower-scented garden and thought how different it all was from smoky Rossendale. A part of me wished that I could stay for ever in beautiful Worcester and have a wonderful life with Uncle and Betty. But I had to go home.

On the last day of my holiday, the owner of the hat shop gave me £2 in payment for my help! I had never dreamed of being paid; helping Betty had been such a pleasure for me.

I ran to a shoe shop and bought the red and black wedge-heeled shoes I had seen in the window and longed to have.

That evening, when I sat with Uncle and Betty in the garden, I told them how greatly I had enjoyed my stay. Uncle said, 'How would you like to come and live here with us? You shouldn't be working in a mill; I'd get you a proper job – something with training and prospects.' I was amazed! My thoughts of living with Uncle and Betty had been castles in the air. But now it could all come true. Then a thought struck me: Uncle wanted me, but what about Betty? I turned to her; she was nodding and smiling at me, so I knew that she too wanted me.

'I'm not pushing you,' Uncle assured me. 'Don't decide now. Think about it for a month. Whatever you decide will be all right.'

The next day Uncle saw me off at the station. As the train sped north, it seemed to be carrying me away from a world filled with warmth and sunlight.

I can't remember what Dad said when I got home and announced that Uncle wanted me to go and live with him and Betty. But I vividly remember Mother's reaction. When Dad wasn't there she told me, 'Your precious uncle only wants you because you are earning a wage.' I knew that Mother didn't like Uncle, but I was absolutely stunned by her vicious interpretation of his motive as a way of making money out of me. For her to say such a thing about my generous uncle who wanted only to give to me, and who cared about my future, was beyond belief!

'That's rich, coming from you,' I cried. 'You're the one who only wants me for my wage!'

She gibbered with rage and exploded, 'If you go, you can't come back and you'll never see your father again.'

I told her, 'No one but you could come up with such absurd rubbish, but then,' I taunted, 'you're not very bright, are you?'

That tore it. She snatched a pint pot from the table and smashed it through a glass panel in the bookcase. 'Temper, temper,' I mocked, then I flounced off to work.

Dad replaced the glass panel. I don't know Mother's version of what had happened but, whatever it was, Dad never said anything about it to me, so I didn't say a word.

I don't know why I kept quiet. Perhaps I was absorbed in considering whether or not I should go to Worcester. I was very tempted, but in the end I didn't go. Despite the attraction of being with Uncle and Betty, and getting away from the mill, I couldn't part from Ted and my youth club; I just couldn't.

I didn't see busy Ted very often, but I went to the club most evenings. It was run by our two leaders, Mr Slater, my ex-schoolteacher, and Mr Schofield, another teacher. Mr Slater was also headmaster of the night school held in the same school building. Attendance at two classes was a qualification for youth club membership. Mr Slater was very strict about this rule; he chased up people who tried to get away with only going to the club.

There were technical and practical classes for the boys, dressmaking and shorthand with bookkeeping for the girls. I was not interested in sewing or clerical know-how, but I enjoyed learning shorthand. Classes ended at nine o'clock, so there was plenty of time left for dancing and table tennis.

I took part in many club activities: at a table tennis inter-club match I won a silver medal. And I played various roles in dramatic productions for area competitions that our group often won. There were rambles, weekend youth hostelling expeditions and dances.

Our leaders were fully committed to us; they must have put in many unpaid hours on our behalf and our debt to them is enormous; they gave us our youth and many happy memories to look back on in later years.

They would certainly not have approved of something I longed to take part in, which had nothing to do with the club activities.

At that time, all night parties were very popular. Of course I was not allowed to stay out all night; I had to be home by eleven. I had once, and only once, got home from a dance at midnight. I had dared to be so late only because Dad would not be in; it was his fire-watching night. All males had to spend a weekly night sleeping at their place of employment in case incendiary bombs were dropped during an air raid. Unfortunately for me, Dad had swapped nights with someone; when I got home he was there and absolutely beside himself with fury.

He shouted, even swore at me and slapped my face, sending my glasses flying. I'd never heard Dad swear; I don't know which frightened me most: his angry 'bloody' or the hard slap. But frightened I most certainly was.

Nevertheless, with a bit of devious plotting, it wasn't long before I managed to stay all night at a party. One of my friends, Lena, asked me to stay with her one Saturday night. Her mother was going to visit her army husband stationed in the south. I explained to Dad that Lena was afraid to sleep alone in the house and got his permission to stay with her overnight.

'Great!' I told Lena. 'We'll have an all night party.' She wasn't keen, but I talked her round. A crowd from the youth club, plus Ted, came. We played kissing games. The first was Rugby – it got its name from the rough scrums that took place on the floor. We sat in a circle: each of us had a number, even for the girls and odd for the boys. The ball, played by a girl, sat mid-circle and called out several boys' numbers; they hurled themselves at the ball and struggled to be the first to kiss her. The winner then took her place and the process was reversed. Before playing Rugby, girls always took off their stockings; you had to give two of your precious clothing ration coupons per pair, so laddered stockings were a disaster that nobody could afford. Other games such as Murder and Sardines took place in the dark with plenty of opportunity for kissing, so a good time was had by all.

In the early hours of the morning, people drifted away or fell asleep on the floor. Ted had to go; he was due on Home Guard parade at six o'clock for an anti-invasion exercise.

I walked with him to the town centre. We kissed each other goodnight and went our separate ways. I set off back to Lena's house with the intention of getting some sleep. The streets were pitch-dark and there wasn't a soul about as I scurried over the railway crossing. Suddenly a voice shouted, 'Hey!' I stopped and looked round. A policeman on a bike whizzed up beside me.

'What are you doing here?' he demanded. 'Where are you going?' I gasped out a frightened explanation and said that I was going to my friend's house. He produced a notebook and snapped, 'Your name and address.'

Terror gripped me at the prospect of what would happen if the policeman told Dad that I'd been found on the streets at night. I thought fast and gave the policeman a false name and address. He wrote it all down and asked for my identity card. I was appalled! My identity card, a wartime security measure, bore my true name and address. 'It's at home,' I babbled in panic. He told me to produce it at the police station within forty-eight hours, and then he rode off.

If I had given the policeman my true name and address and presented my identity card at the police station, it would have been the end of the matter. But my stupid lies had made that impossible; I could not produce a card with my invented details.

For several days I lived on tenterhooks, trying to persuade myself that nothing was going to happen. Of course, it did. I was walking home from the club when I saw the policeman riding towards me on his bike. I knew straight away that he was coming for me. I stopped as he drew level and got off his bike.

It hadn't taken him long to track me down after the forty-eight hours had expired. My false name and address had been such a panic-stricken mixture of truth and invention that investigation had soon revealed my identity. To my horror he said, 'I've seen your father. I informed him that you will be charged with two offences: giving a false name and address, and failing to produce an identity card.' I reeled with shock. I'd had no idea that I had broken the law!

After the policeman had gone, I walked slowly towards home. All hell was going to be let loose. I wanted to run away, but where could I could I go? To Uncle Lennie? But I had no money for the train fare. There was nothing for it but to go home and face the music.

Chapter 15

When I trailed in through the door Dad wasn't there; he'd gone fire watching, but Mother was waiting with steam up. 'A policeman's been here for you.'

'I know,' I said miserably.

She let rip with a furious tirade: what I had done would bring shame on the family, there would be a report in the *Free Press*: 'Local preacher's daughter had up in court', everybody would know. 'Your father will never be able to hold his head up again.'

I was devastated. I knew that Dad preached in churches all over the valley, but it had not occurred to me that what I had done could affect him. I crept off to bed and cried myself to sleep.

When I woke up the next morning, it all hit me straight away. I went downstairs. Dad was back. He didn't go for me, but if he had knocked me to the floor it would have been easier to bear than his quiet reproach, 'You've let me down again.' I burst into tears.

'You'd better tell me exactly what happened.' I told him about the party and my encounter with the policeman. 'Why did you give him a false name and address?' I sobbed out that I'd been frightened of what he would do if the policeman told him that I'd been on the streets at night.

When I had calmed down he told me, 'The policeman is coming to take a statement from you, tonight. You'll be all right,' he assured me, 'I'll be here. Whatever he asks, just tell him the truth.'

I got home from work after a dreadful day of worry; Dad wasn't in. Mother ignored me as I sat, taut with fear, waiting for the policeman to arrive, but he didn't come.

When Dad came in he said, 'I've been to the police station. I saw the chief constable; I told him I'm to blame for what happened and that you lied because you were frightened of me. I asked him to put the onus on me. He said he would consider the matter.'

Several fraught days went by with both of us worrying. It was all we could think about. I felt terrible when Dad said, 'I wonder whether the chief constable has children; if he has, perhaps he'll think how he would feel if he was in my position.' Of course I knew that Dad's concern was not for himself: he was worried sick about what might happen to me if the magistrates at the court hearing decided that I was out of parental control.

At last a letter came from the chief constable; Dad handed it to me. It said that no further action would be taken against me on the understanding that in future I would be kept under control. And I was. If I wanted to go anywhere or do anything Dad didn't approve of, he merely took the letter out of his desk and held it before my eyes.

I accepted restriction because I was very grateful indeed to Dad for taking the blame on his own shoulders when it had all been my fault; if I had not disobeyed and deceived him about the all-night party, none of it would have happened.

I felt tremendously guilty for causing so much trouble and did my best to make amends. To show that I was making a real effort to improve, I even tried to please Mother by being pleasant and helpful. But her inimical refusal to respond to my overtures daily reaffirmed my disgrace and reinforced my guilt. She made it plain that what I had done was unforgivable. 'Mine, right or wrong, mine,' was not something that my stepmother could feel for me.

But when all is said and done, being stuck with me must have been difficult for her. Perhaps our relationship might have been better had I been a quiet, biddable child and a well-behaved teenager, but I was neither. In fact, as I had become increasingly articulate in my teens, I had certainly made things worse by easily getting the better of Mother in our verbal flare-ups. But my disgrace had put her in the superior position; I no longer had a leg to stand on should conflict arise. Not that it did. I was a pariah, so I kept quiet and endured my doghouse existence.

As the days passed I began to wish that I could find somewhere else to live; somewhere not too far away from Ted and my youth club. I went to the Labour Exchange to see if any maids were required at the big houses. I didn't mind what I did if it got me away from home – and the mill. I told myself that if I was offered a job I would take it and nobody was going to stop me.

The clerk at the Exchange was helpful when I asked about live-in jobs. She said, 'There's nothing at the moment, but if you don't mind leaving home you could become a student nurse. There's a shortage of nurses in several hospitals near Manchester.'

I seized on the prospect with enthusiasm. There was so much in its favour. I could get away from Mother and the mill, and do something really worthwhile; something that would stop me feeling guilty and disgraced.

The clerk promptly rang the hospital I chose from her list and made an appointment for me with the matron. Stepping Hill Hospital was at Stockport, near Manchester, so a couple of bus rides would get me home to my friends on days off.

Dad was pleased when I announced that I wanted to be a

student nurse. The following morning I went for my interview and was accepted for training with the next intake of students.

I gave my notice at the mill and told my pals at the club where I was going. You'd have thought I was going to China; 'You will write, won't you?' everyone said. I pointed out that I'd be home one day a week. Ted was delighted when I told him about my new venture. He said, 'Let me know when you get a day off, then we can arrange to meet.' So I was over the moon, with everything sorted to my satisfaction.

One September morning I presented myself at the hospital's nurses' home, where I was received by Sister Kilner, the briskly efficient and stern home sister. She quick-marched me to my room where she said that I must never sit on the bed as a chair was provided. She told me to put on the black stockings and flat ward shoes I had been instructed to bring, gave me a uniform, showed me how to construct the cap and left me to get changed. Then she came back and marched me to the dining room for a meal.

Barely an hour after my arrival I was on the female 'Chronic' ward, where I was promptly addressed as 'Nurse' – an instant transformation hardly merited by me, as I knew nothing at all about nursing. But that was quickly remedied; I found myself on a 'steep learning curve'.

The ward's twenty beds were occupied by incurably ill patients; most of them were elderly and called grannies. The ward Sister, who looked nearly as old as the grannies, handed me over to a cheerful, buxom Irish nurse called Butler. She showed me how to bed-bath the grannies unable to get in or out of a bath.

I'd had no idea that such awful things could happen to the human body. I was horrified by the pear-shaped reddish bladders protruding like balloons between the legs of several comatose grannies. Nurse Butler told me that the condition was a complete prolapse of the womb. Goodness knows for how long those poor souls had had to live with it, or how many other women were enduring prolapse problems at that time. (When the NHS, with free medical treatment for all, came in after the War, doctors reported large numbers of women with long-standing prolapse problems coming to their surgeries for treatment that they had never been able to afford.)

The day staff went off duty at eight o'clock. We returned to the Home for a good meal with heaped plates. Afterwards, on my way to my room, I met another new nurse; she was in tears. 'I want to go home,' she sobbed. 'I phoned my mum and we both just cried and cried.' I comforted her as well as I could, but I thought how lucky she was to have a mother who cried for her daughter.

Lights out at eleven o'clock plunged the entire Home into complete darkness. In bed, I promptly fell asleep and dreamed all night of scurrying, black-stockinged legs, until a knock on the door and Sister Kilner shouting, 'Ten-to-six, Nurse,' awoke me to my first full day on the ward.

After breakfast, the day staff went in procession across the grounds to the hospital. An overnight accumulation of geriatric incontinence smell met me as I went into the ward. The windows were all bricked up to prevent flying glass from bomb-blasts descending onto patients. A small unbricked space at the top of the windows was opened during the day to air the ward.

Patients were fed; it took ages to feed the helpless grannies. Bottoms were washed and soiled sheets changed at regular intervals throughout the day (there were no incontinence pads then). I rinsed the filthy sheets in the sluice and dumped them in a laundry trolley. Bedpan rounds for patients who could use them were also my job, as was scrubbing out lockers, cupboards and the sluice.

Of course, on my first day I managed to break a rule. It happened when Matron was doing her daily round of the ward. Now, in my experience, when the boss was around you let him/her see that you were working hard, so, when Matron appeared, I got on with making a patient's bed, tucking in the sheets with hospital corners as nurse Butler had taught me. Sister left Matron's side, bustled over to me and hissed, 'Nurse! When Matron is on the ward you must stand to attention at the foot of a bed.'

I stood amazed and embarrassed while Sister escorted Matron round the ward. When they got to me, Matron looked at the bed. Then she gave me a gentle smile, turned to Sister and said, 'Nurse has learned to make a bed very nicely.' In the casual way she said it, there was no hint of criticism of Sister's overreaction to a new nurse's mistake, and instead of censure I received encouragement.

It was no wonder that Matron was liked and respected by everyone. Tall, stately and kind, though very firm, she was nothing like the hated and feared assistant Matron who was known as the Ass-Mat. She was large and intimidating, with bold aggressive eyes and a sergeant-major voice.

The following day, I went with the new intake of students to our first lecture in the study, a cheerful room with green and white check curtains and light oak desks.

Sister Tutor, small, tubby and authoritative, began our instruction with a set of rules. The first was based on the 'no followers' rule that had been laid down for servants in middle or upper-class Victorian households. Like them, we were now in 'no man's land'.

'Boyfriends are not allowed in the Nurses' Home, nor must they wait outside the hospital's entrance.' Other rules included supervision of our comings and goings.

'A nurse is only allowed to sleep away from the hospital with Matron's permission. A sleeping-out pass may be obtained by requesting your ward sister to apply to Matron. A book outside her office must be signed before leaving the hospital.' The latter rule was a justifiable precaution: the book was to be used to check who was absent if the Home were to be hit in an air raid – as had happened at Manchester's Infirmary, when the hospital had been bombed and people killed.

Rules apart, Sister's lectures were interesting and informative. We made notes on how to nurse patients with various illnesses, and we practised bandaging techniques on a dummy called Miss Chaste.

As well as a weekly day off, every nurse had a two-hour off-duty period during the day. There was always a welcoming fire in the nurses' sitting room, but, if you went in there, you risked having to spend your off duty time working in the laundry where they were short-staffed. Matron would appear and gently request volunteers. Reluctant though you were, you could hardly refuse when Matron herself went to the laundry with her nurses and stood feeding sheets into rollers.

The hospital was largely staffed by Irish nurses, many of whom came from poor rural areas where unemployment and large families to feed meant that girls had to come to England for work. Some nurses had followed older sisters, cousins or friends to Stepping Hill, so they had the comfort of being with their own kind during the long separation from home. They lived for their annual long leave. When a nurse returned, she must have brought back with her the very breath of Ireland to the nurses gathered in her room to hear the news from home.

Naturally they clung together, but they were not exclusive; lively and out-going, they were always ready for high-jinks. Nurses Butler and Heggerty taught me to dance an Irish jig and I taught them to jitterbug. This was during the ward's visiting hours, when Sister was busy in the kitchen with visitors' enquiries and we were in the bathroom supposedly scrubbing rubber incontinence sheets; we just wiped them with a damp cloth then, from their damp appearance, Sister would assume that they had been scrubbed. When the local Catholic priest came to visit patients on our ward, Butler and Heggerty went into ecstasies, partly because he was their own Irish priest but mostly because he was, as young people say now, 'dead gorgeous'. Alas for my friends, Father Flynn was no girl's land.

One evening I went to the cinema with Butler and Heggerty to see *Going My Way*, in which the popular star, Bing Crosby, played a charismatic Catholic priest.

I was as keen as most teenagers were on Bing, but his priest role meant little to me because I was only a Sunday morning Catholic. This was greatly to my advantage, as I had discovered, during my first week on the ward, when Sister had made up the off duty rota. For some reason she had assumed that I was a Catholic and put me down for the Sunday seven o'clock – ten o'clock off duty period that the Catholic nurses got so that they could go to Mass. I didn't put her wise because a Sunday seven to ten gave me two nights away instead of one. Along with the other new nurses I got Saturday for my day off, so I could leave the hospital on Friday evening and return by ten o'clock on Sunday. Thus my Catholic status gave me Friday evenings of dancing etc. at the youth club, with all the pleasures of Saturday evening – and maybe a date with Ted – in prospect.

The fares for my weekly journeys left me very hard up. My monthly pay was two pounds seven shillings. I spent two nights at home, so I had to cough up my pay. Mother gave me the same four shillings a week spending money I had been given when I worked at the mill. Bus fares then had never cost more than a few pence because I walked almost everywhere, so I'd always had something to spend.

But now fares took most of my money, and being hard up presented a problem when Christmas came near.

One December morning Sister told me, 'Nurse, there's a parcel for you in the kitchen.'

It had come by registered post, so it was delivered to the ward. Inside my parcel was a box with a jeweller's name on the lid. Inside was a pretty necklace from Ted. I was both thrilled and dismayed. How on earth was I going to buy a Christmas present for him when I had so little money? My problem was solved, but not entirely to my satisfaction: Mother sold me a scarf at a reduced price from her shop. It was a warm, good quality scarf but it was a dull brown colour. I wished that I could have given Ted something more exciting than a dreary scarf. But when I gave it to him on our next date he said, 'Oh! Thank you. I haven't got a scarf,' and wore it straight away.

I wore my new necklace at the staff Christmas party held by Matron. Some party! Matron sat smiling benevolently as a nurse recited heart-rending Victorian ballads: 'The Little Match Girl' and 'The Crossing Sweeper', and someone sang 'Going Home', which made the Irish nurses cry. After Matron had gone, we danced to gramophone records. There was only one male partner to go round – a boy who worked in the maintenance department. He had a good time with a red-haired nurse and the rest of us danced with each other.

On Christmas Eve, nurses and domestic staff walked in procession through the darkened wards singing carols, with Matron leading the way and carrying a lamp – like Florence Nightingale. In ward after ward, medical, surgical, maternity and others, there were faces on pillows and eyes shining in the lamplight as we passed.

We all, including the patients, enjoyed that lovely celebration of Christmas.

Chapter 16

On Christmas Day, in keeping with hospital tradition, there was no off duty but everything was unusually relaxed. A delicious buffet was set out in the dining room and the Mayor of Stockport had sent dozens of gorgeous cakes.

All the wards were open, so you could go into any ward and chat to the patients. The only closed ward was the one in which some German prisoners of war were being nursed. No doubt they would have enjoyed a visit – so would we, had it been allowed – but only very senior nurses who worked on the Germans' ward could visit.

There wasn't much Christmas celebration on the chronic ward. Most of the grannies didn't even know it was Christmas; they lay with eyes closed, drifting peacefully towards death.

Someone brought in a very old man to visit his wife. He stood totally bewildered in the doorway. I asked him for his wife's name and took him to her bed. But he shook his head. He couldn't recognise his wife. Probably she had greatly changed since he had last seen her, and she was past recognising anybody. I could not convince him that Granny Holden was his wife, so he wandered from bed to bed, peering at the grannies, until his escort came to collect him. It was very sad.

I made the most of Christmas Day freedom to talk to patients on our ward. Normally this was not permitted because Sister thought that talking to patients was a waste of time when you could be scrubbing something.

Not all the patients were senile. There was Mrs Shaw, a nice old lady who was dying from cancer. She was very lonely and desperate for human contact, so I used to talk to her whenever I got the chance. But Sister would send me off with, 'Nurse! We haven't got time to talk. Go and scrub out the lockers,' or something else I'd scrubbed on the previous day. This infuriated me. I thought it cruel to deprive a lonely old lady of a bit of comfort.

One day Mrs Shaw told me, 'You are my friend, so may I call you Betty?' But when Sister heard Mrs Shaw call me by my name we were both told off for undermining ward discipline. Mrs Shaw was very upset because she thought she'd got me into trouble.

Sister's dismissal of patients' emotional needs certainly did not reflect something that Matron had told us new nurses: 'Always remember that this hospital is for the benefit of the patients.'

But no doubt Sister was right about one thing. When she caught me shedding tears in the sluice after Mrs Shaw died, she told me, 'You will have to get used to death.' Of course, a nurse must not become too emotionally involved with a patient, but, at the age of seventeen, I was incapable of that necessary detachment.

Nor could I shrug off, as older nurses did, the blame I got for things that were not my fault. One day a very confused patient used her sweet ration coupons instead of toilet paper. There would have been no point in fishing filthy coupons out of the bedpan, so I'd bunged the lot down the sluice. When the patient's daughter reported the missing coupons to Sister and insisted that they must have been stolen by a nurse, I revealed their fate and copped it for failing to stop the patient using the coupons that I didn't even know were in her handbag.

Another day found me in worse trouble. The Ass-Mat was doing a ward round when a stentorian bellow, 'Nurse!'

summoned me to Mrs Russell's bed. To my horror, the Ass-Mat was pointing to a stinking bedpan on the locker. I knew what had happened. Mrs Russell often hid a bedpan beneath her bedclothes and dumped it on the locker after use. This was not because she wanted to get me into trouble; she was just making sure that she'd always got a bedpan on tap. The Ass-Mat gave me no opportunity to explain, so I just bowed before the storm. And storm she did! After she'd gone, I got another blast from Sister.

I was fed up with being in trouble. Furthermore, I had got a sharp pain beneath my right shoulder blade, which I thought was caused by lifting helpless patients. Normally two nurses lifted and turned patients; but we were very short-staffed, so it was often a one-nurse job. I thought that the pain would go away in time, but it got worse.

Then I caught scabies, a skin parasite that causes intense irritation. Other nurses caught it too. There was an outbreak of scabies during the War, but, at the time, none of us knew what we'd got. We itched and scratched from morning till night. The only relief was to take a hot bath before going to bed. Fortunately there was plenty of hot water; it was so hot that we used to make cocoa from the bath taps.

Nobody fancied reporting itchy skin to Sister Kilner. One nurse had gone to her with a boil and been told that it was her own fault for not keeping herself clean. Kilner had no patience with nurses' complaints, so there was no point in telling her that I'd got a pain in my back.

Then, much to my dismay, my day off was changed from Saturday to Wednesday. Ted and I had met at the youth club on the Saturdays when he wasn't doing magic shows, but weeknight meetings were impossible. During the week he was busy with course work and various events that he organized for the Students' Union. Anyway, I had to return to the hospital on Wednesday evening to be on duty next morning at seven o'clock. But at least on my brief visits home I could see my dad; he was always very glad to see me.

I wrote to Ted and explained what had happened, but no reply came. Every morning I hoped for a letter when I scurried to the Home, where piles of toast and bowls of butter were set out in the dining room for our mid-morning sustenance. I hastily scanned the letters on the post table. Sometimes there was a welcome letter from Uncle Lennie, but nothing from Ted.

The next thing to happen was the cancellation of sleeping out passes when nighttime air raids began again. I ignored the cancellation and went home. I was glad that I had. The next morning when I got up I found Dad in the kitchen in the throes of a severe asthma attack. He was blue in the face, gasping for breath and unable to speak. I went into action with the treatment I had learned at the hospital. I hastily boiled the kettle until steam was coming from the spout, then I put a towel over Dad's head and told him to inhale the steam. Within minutes he was breathing normally. He was relieved and very grateful. 'Now I know what to do when I have an attack.' Then he gave me half-a-crown.

Sister Kilner was waiting for me when I returned to the hospital that evening. 'Nurse, did you sleep out last night?'

'Yes, Sister.'

'Don't do it again or I shall report you to Matron.' So I was stuck at the hospital for who knew how long.

Back on the ward I struggled to work with my painful back giving me gyp. Constant pain is debilitating, so I felt very tired; and the skin on my arms was inflamed and sore from scratching the perpetual itch.

Now that I couldn't go home to see my friends and Dad, I felt trapped. Worst of all was my loss of contact with Ted. Why didn't he write? Had he got someone else? I grew more and more depressed. Then one Sunday everything came to a head.

That morning Mrs Russell, all smiles, showed me a postcard. It was from her son to say that he would be coming to see her in the afternoon. I was very glad for her. Neither her son nor anyone else ever visited Mrs Russell, so it was a great day for her.

Visiting time came. Mrs Russell anxiously watched the door as visitors began to trickle into the ward. Sister sent me to scrub bedpans in the sluice. Every few minutes I popped my head round the door to see whether Mrs Russell's son had arrived, but there was no sign of him. Mrs Russell was still watching the door.

At three o'clock I helped to serve the patients their Sunday treat of fruit slab cake and tea. Mrs Russell didn't want any; her agonised gaze was still riveted on the door. I could have strangled her wretched son when the bell rang, ending visiting time and Mrs Russell's hopes. She cried as if her heart was broken.

I sat beside her on the bed so that I could put my arm round her and try to comfort her. Sister arrived. 'Nurse! What are you doing? You know that a nurse is not allowed to sit on a patient's bed.' I protested that I was trying to comfort Mrs Russell; but I should have known that a patient's misery would not be allowed to interfere with Sister's inexorable ward routine; she sent me to wash up the tea crockery in the kitchen.

I stood at the sink, crying into the washing up. Nothing was going right. Everything was piling up on me: the constant trouble I was in; the pain in my back; my itching, burning skin; and the cancellation of sleeping out passes that had isolated me from my friends at the club and any hope of seeing Ted.

Suddenly I felt totally unable to cope with it all any longer. When I went off duty I went to my room, packed my case and left without a word to anyone.

I have since often regretted my action, but, at that time, I wasn't thinking straight. I just wanted to get away.

When I got home, Dad was there. He was dismayed when I told him that I wasn't going back to the hospital. But when I had poured out my woes and showed him my inflamed arms he said, 'You should have come home before now.'

When Mother came in, she looked at my arms. 'You've got scabies; it's very infectious.' Naturally she was concerned that it might spread round the family, so the next morning she took me to Dr Lees.

He confirmed that I'd got scabies. 'You must go to the clinic for treatment,' he said. Then he examined me all over including my back. 'Oh, look at this!' He turned to Mother, told her that my right shoulder blade was displaced and that he would arrange for me to see a consultant in Manchester.

I went to the clinic for scabies treatment. My skin was painted with something that made it purple. It soon cleared up the infection, but I felt too tired and dispirited to do anything but sleep.

When my appointment with the orthopaedic consultant arrived, Mother and Dad went with me. The consultant was very kind. He asked, 'When did you first feel pain in your back?' I told him about the ache that had started when I was working on the skiver, and that it had got very painful when I was nursing. He said that both jobs had probably made my condition worse because I had greenstick bones (I was still growing), but they had not actually caused it. He also said that lifting heavy weights was something I should avoid, so nursing was not for me.

He didn't give any more information; patients were told very little in those days. It was to be years before I learned that I had got scoliosis, curvature of the spine, which usually appears during adolescence and is thought to be hereditary. Dad paid five pounds for the consultation, which was probably as much, if not more, than he earned in a week.

Subsequently I was sent to an orthopaedic clinic in Haslingden, where I was given weekly radiant heat treatment and exercises to do at home. The pain went away and I began to feel much better.

Dad found me a job with another of his insurance clients. Mr Taylor had a small bakery behind a shop on the road running along the valley bottom. Work started at seven o'clock in the back room, where a large oven took up most of the space.

The first job of the day was meat pie making. Mr Taylor showed me how to pop blobs of pastry into small tins, which were then placed on a moulding block. A lever was pulled down and the tins were promptly lined with pastry ready for filling with mincemeat and cereal. Although the pie lids had to be rolled and stamped out by hand, the moulding machine enabled the swift production of dozens of pies for the local mill workers' mid-morning break.

For the rest of the day I helped to make bread, teacakes and cakes for the shop. I was given a very good dinner by Mrs Taylor. As soon as I had eaten it, I was back on the job, so it was a long day in that hot little room without a proper break. But I enjoyed baking and Mr Taylor, who was a master baker, taught me a great deal.

Back at my youth club I kept an eye open for Ted, but he didn't appear or get in touch. Then I heard that he was going out with a girl from his college. I told myself I didn't care. Of course I did. But I wasn't too cast down; freed from the hospital's strict regime, I was thoroughly enjoying myself; and, now that I wasn't going out with Ted, I made the most of my opportunities.

As well as walking home from the club with various boys, I went to the cinema with lads home on leave from the forces. Dad was not pleased when, on his way to fire watching, he encountered me with different escorts. And he viewed with suspicion the letters I received from lads who were away. We girls made sure that they got the youth club magazines to keep them in touch with home. Sometimes they sent back accounts of life in the forces, which were included in the magazine, plus news garnered from letters received by other girls. Sometimes there was very sad news.

One Sunday I went to sing with the club's choir at a memorial service for a lad I'd danced with only a few weeks before, when he'd been on leave from the navy. He and many others had died when their ship was sunk by a German U-boat.

The heart-rending grief of his parents left its mark on me. I asked myself, *what if this should one day happen to me?* I hoped that I would never have a son.

Now that I was back at home, I was again doing the housework. Of course, on my return Mother hadn't received me with open arms, but she had stopped giving me the pariah treatment. No doubt, after months of doing the housework herself, she was glad enough to hand it back to me. I didn't mind; I could easily whip round our small house in an hour and then catch a later bus to the club.

This didn't satisfy Mother at all. In her view, I wasn't doing enough to justify my place in the household, so one evening, when I'd cleaned up and was about to head off to the club, she told me to scrub the cellar steps and white donkey-stone the edges – a procedure normally confined to front door steps. Nobody dreamed of scrubbing a flight of stone stairs leading to a coal cellar. I was certainly not going to do it, so I told her to get lost. In the ensuing row she picked up a plate, banged it on the table till it broke and burst into tears.

At that moment, Dad walked in. 'What's the matter?' I told him, then I left them to sort it out. I don't know what was said, but from that time on Dad intervened on my behalf whenever Mother made unreasonable demands. When she decided that I was to do the family's washing on Sunday mornings, he put his foot down. In those days there were no washing machines, so it all had to be done by hand and took hours of hard work, which was why Mother had often kept me off school to do it. But now Dad said that, after six days of early rising for work, I needed a lie-in on Sunday mornings, and no more was said.

Mother continually found fault with my cleaning up; one day Dad suggested that she might try a bit of praise instead of criticism. Another time, when I was scrubbing the petty seat, the brush slipped from my soapy hand and vanished down the hole. 'You'll pay three pence for that brush,' Mother snapped.

'Just a moment,' Dad said, 'it was an accident so that wouldn't be fair.'

I wonder now whether all this was causing conflict between Dad and Mother. Of course there could have been other reasons why she was giving him a hard time, with nightly nagging sessions after my siblings and I had gone to bed. The thick walls muffled sound, but I could hear her angry voice going on and on, so obviously something was wrong. Not that I cared about their relationship, or what went on at home; it was merely the place where I slept. I just lived for dancing with my new boyfriend, Dave.

One night at the club he'd asked me for a dance. We glided round the room to Glen Miller's 'Moonlight Serenade'; our steps matched perfectly and we moved as one. For the rest of the evening we danced on cloud nine, then he took me home.

It had gone on from there and now Dave was in the throes of first love. He sent me letters and poems and even waited outside the bakery every day to walk me home. It was very flattering to have someone in love with me, especially now that Ted no longer wanted me. Emotionally insecure as ever, I was ready to love anyone who loved me, so, in a way, I loved Dave.

We were both obsessed with dancing. Oh, how we danced! Almost every night we quickstepped, waltzed and jitterbugged.

Dad complained that I thought of nothing but dancing. He was right. But after all, youth is the time to dance. And now that it is no longer the time to dance (you can't do much dancing on a walking stick), I have no regrets. Although I do greatly regret something I did one night when I was getting ready to go dancing with Dave.

Dad was watching me combing my hair at the mirror. Suddenly he said how nice it would be if I were to spend an evening at home for a change. Sixty years later, a sharp pang goes through me whenever I remember what I did then. I flung myself down on a chair and sat scowling for all I was worth until, in the end, Dad said sadly, 'If that's the way you feel, you might as well go.' I leapt up, grabbed my coat and rushed through the door.

Well, what would I give now for an evening, an hour, with my dad.

My lay-preacher dad who tried and failed to keep me unsoiled by the world.

Emily, my real mother. The portrait I stole from dad.

Aged fourteen and still a child. My Wakes Week Blackpool holiday from the mill.

Aged eighteen, on a bad hair day.

Ted the magician. Boxes, alarm clocks, silks and a rabbit come out of a top hat.

Youth hostelling and courting in Derbyshire.

Youth House in Camden Town, London, on the day of the Spring Fair when Joe's lost snake made an unexpected appearance.

*My mother-in-law, Martha, in borrowed finery.
She could never afford any new clothes.*

Our wedding day in 1947. 'Together for always, now.'

1966. Ted and I with our five children. The real family I had always longed to have.

Chapter 17

In May 1945, the war with Germany ended. Hitler, trapped in a Berlin bunker with the allies closing in, committed suicide and Germany surrendered. I had been twelve years old when the war started; when it ended I was eighteen.

VE day (victory in Europe; Japan surrendered a few weeks later) was declared a national holiday. In the afternoon, Dave and I walked on the hills and heard brass bands trumpeting victory from towns and villages across the valley. In the evening we joined our friends and took part in the general celebration. What a night that was! We were caught up in a heady whirl of excitement that sent us racing madly up onto the hills where, when it got dark, we looked down on the valley marvellously ablaze with light, now that the blackout had ended.

In the town centre, hundreds of people had gathered. Garlands of coloured lights sparkled in the trees in the nearby park, and dance music was blasting from a radiogram and loud speakers set up on a platform, round which a huge crowd was dancing. We ran down to join them and danced up a storm. I wore out the soles of my shoes dancing on the stone setts.

Shortly after the War ended, the national newspapers were filled with reports of the horrors found by allied troops when they liberated the Nazi concentration camps.

At the club, our group sat together in the quiet room, where members could read magazines and play board games. We were stunned by the papers' revelations. It seemed beyond belief that anyone could treat people with such cruelty. But we concluded that it must be true, because nobody could have invented something so monstrous. And, although we had known nothing of the camps, we felt a sense of guilt with the realisation that, whilst we had been enjoying our happy, carefree lives, people had been undergoing such appalling suffering.

Little did I know then that, in the near future, I was to become involved with some lonely young refugees from Nazi oppression.

The weeks passed; Dave and I danced the summer away, went hostelling with our friends in Derbyshire and played in table tennis matches. When September came, Dave decided that he wanted to be a teacher and went off to a college in Yorkshire. We wrote to each other; he was enjoying college life and making new friends, but I felt bereft without him.

I joined an evening school Esperanto class taught by an elderly white-bearded professor. Esperanto is an international language. The professor said that it was going to open up communication between people of all races and tongues. It was a good idea but, as far as I know, it has never really taken off.

One evening when I emerged from the class, I got a shock. Ted was standing there smiling at me. My heart turned over but I kept my cool. 'Hello, stranger.'

He looked embarrassed. 'I've been busy with exams.' Over coffee in the canteen he told me that he'd got his degree and started work in a Manchester textile research and development centre.

Despite my attachment to Dave, I'd never stopped hoping that Ted would come back, but, now that he had, I was in a whirl. Part of me was over the moon; all the same I told myself that if he thought he could just walk back into my life and find me waiting, he'd got another thing coming. So when he asked me to go with him to the cinema I said, 'Sorry, I've got another boyfriend.' Nor would I let him take me home. He kept appearing at the club looking forlorn. When that didn't work, he started talking animatedly to other girls. He was probably trying to make me jealous. I was. Before long I gave way and started going to the cinema with him.

I knew I should tell Dave that I was seeing Ted, but I didn't. The reason was not to my credit: I needed to hang on to Dave because I didn't want Ted to think he was the only pebble on the beach. I let him know that I was keeping up my relationship with Dave. I even told him that I wouldn't be able to see him when Dave came home for Christmas. I got my comeuppance for that.

When Dave came home, he dumped me. He'd moved on into college life and lost interest in me. Well, it's what usually happens; students' home attachments do get left behind. Anyway, I spent a miserable Christmas without Dave or Ted, which served me right.

But that was the end of my silly capricious behaviour. Ted and I soon got back on our old footing. Before long we were together most evenings; and I knew that we belonged to each other in a way that Dave and I never had or ever could. And I needed to belong, to love and be loved.

Ted wasn't as keen as I was on dancing, but we often went to the Astoria and waltzed dreamily beneath a revolving ceiling light casting misty drifts of colour over walls and dancers. On Saturdays when Ted was booked to do a magic show, I went with him. After his performance I helped backstage to pack the magical gear in two enormous cases.

I became quite caught up in the mystery of magic, so when Ted asked me to be his on-stage assistant, I agreed. He said, 'Come to tea at my house tomorrow and I'll show you the ropes.'

I did not look forward to meeting Ted's family; I was sure that they wouldn't think much of me, so I was filled with apprehension when I knocked on the door of their terrace house. There was a great outburst of barking. Ted opened the door and two enormous greyhounds came hurtling up the passage.

The dogs were banished to the back yard and Ted introduced me to his family. His father, Tom, had a thick thatch of grey hair and a thin, weary face. He spoke the old Lancashire dialect common to his generation and was very deaf from years of work in the din of a cotton mill. His wife, Martha, was small and plump, with greying hair worn in a bun. She looked worn and sad. Their elder son, Cliff, was a shorter version of Ted. Daughter, Doris, was the same age as me and had her brothers' dark good looks.

We all shook hands, then we sat down to tea. As in most mill workers' living rooms, there was a large table, sideboard and chairs, and a ceiling rack hung with clothes. Much to my relief, I was not expected to talk, because we listened to a comedy programme on the wireless as we ate cold sliced beef, pickled onions and stewed figs with custard.

'Flamin' fig seeds,' Tom groaned disgustedly as he rushed to rinse his dentures under the kitchen tap.

After tea I helped to wash up, then Ted took me into the front room and my magic training began. First I had to promise never to reveal the closely guarded secrets of magic. The more I learned about the 'effects', as tricks were called, the more I marvelled at the way in which magicians got away with the things they did. So, the first time I appeared on stage, I was on pins; I was sure that the audience would spot my surreptitious moves, but attention was focussed on the magician, so my undercover activities went unnoticed.

Ted always did shows in formal evening dress, so, from somewhere, he got a long white dress for me to wear. I wasn't allowed to take it home because his mother told us that it wasn't done for a boy to give a dress to a girl. But the dress was only part of the gear needed on stage, so it was hardly a breach of etiquette. However, Martha's view of what was not acceptable, especially where clothes were concerned, was locked into the past. After I turned up wearing slacks, which most girls wore, she told Ted that she didn't approve of me wearing trousers.

As time went by, I was often at her house, helping Ted to prepare for the next show. To some extent she accepted me as Ted's girl, although that had not been the case when I first appeared on the scene. Indeed, I had not expected to be accepted. I was well aware of valley insularity, especially amongst the older generation. If you had not been born and bred in the valley, you were an outsider. My birthplace, Blackpool, was twenty miles away, so I might as well have come from another planet. Furthermore, difference in religious persuasion was frowned upon. The Barnes family attended the local parish church; we were Baptists. I once heard a man at the mill complain that his son was marrying into a family of Baptist buggers, so being one of them was not to my advantage.

But my chief drawback, as far as Martha was concerned, was my lack of education. Her three children had gone to the grammar school; Doris was still there and her brothers had eventually gone on to further education. The fact that I was not well educated must have been difficult for Martha to understand. At the time, she knew nothing of my home life, and, even had she known that my parents' financial problems had limited my education, it would have made no difference because in her book, no matter how hard up you were, you had to give your children a good education.

It wasn't long before I learned that, without Martha's determination and self-sacrifice, her children would have had to go to the mill instead of the grammar school because her husband had always kept her very short of money.

Tom was completely selfish and had absolutely no sense of responsibility for his family. He wasn't lazy; he worked hard at the mill and earned a good wage, but most of it was gambled away at the Blackburn dog track, where he raced his greyhounds every Saturday. Cliff went too. He was a popular, lively lad and full of fun. He had a good job in a laboratory; but he was just like his father, so the bookies got his wages too. I happened to be there one Saturday when they came home from the track.

Martha greeted them, her face tense with hope. 'Did you win?' They shook their heads. Poor Martha flung her hands away in a gesture of despair and resignation. And Cliff borrowed half-a-crown from Ted.

I could see that they all depended on Ted. He did his best for them all, but he resented his father's selfish gambling and the worry it caused his mother. One day he told me just how badly it had undermined the family's welfare.

As children, they had gone short of food. Racing dogs had to be kept in prime condition, so they ate meat whilst the family lived on bread and potatoes. After school medical examinations, Martha had been informed that her children were undernourished, so they were to be given free milk at school.

Eventually, she had got into debt and shopkeepers refused to allow her any more goods on tick. In desperation, she'd got a job in a mill. Tom was furious. Her job was to look after him. 'Anyway,' Ted said, 'he liked to boast to his workmates that his wife didn't need to work because he kept her well provided for – as if the whole town didn't know that she was up to her eyes in debt.'

Martha's job had lasted for just two weeks. 'I'll cure her,' Tom told the children. He ordered that when they got in from school they were to do 'nowt' to help their mother. So, after a long, hard day at the mill, she had wearily come home to yesterday's ashes in the fireless grate, dirty pots on the table, no preparation made for a meal, not even a kettle boiled for a cup of tea. After a week of struggling to cope, Martha gave her notice at the mill. Tom had won.

Naturally, as Ted had told me about his problematic background, I had told him about the ongoing conflict between me and my stepmother. So, when he was invited to our house for tea, he was well prepared for what happened.

I hadn't wanted to ask him to tea. But I was embarrassed about the number of times I'd had tea at his house, so, when Dad said that I really must ask him back, I did.

Dad made him welcome. Mother said nothing and disappeared to the kitchen. I set the table, then I sat beside Ted on the settee. Suddenly Mother shouted from the kitchen, 'Who's left this mess in the sink? Betty – as usual.'

Ted turned to me and said loudly, so that Mother could hear, 'Proper little black sheep, aren't you?' I shot a glance at Dad; he was smiling all over his face! So Ted's humorous defence of me had obviously gone down well with Dad.

In fact, any future attempt on Mother's part to put me down in Ted's eyes was to be undercut with a barbed shaft of humour, which showed her that she was whetting her tongue to no effect.

Somehow she had got the impression that Ted's family was well off (I had not said anything at home about their affairs). She was probably green with envy at the prospect of me marrying into wealth when, one day, she told me, 'You only go to their house because they've got money.' I laughed at the thought of the shock she'd get when she discovered that the Barnes family was harder up than we were.

When Easter came, Ted and I went youth hostelling in Derbyshire. The hills are a superb backdrop to courtship and now, with time to be on our own and talk as we sat on the hilltops, our love for each other deepened.

One day we sheltered from heavy rain at a small railway halt in Hathersage. There wasn't a soul around and no trains came as we sat holding each other close in the rain-drummed waiting room, with surrounding mist and crowding trees on the embankment enclosing us in our own intimate little world. And that was where we decided that we were going to be married and spend the rest of our lives together. 'We'll have to wait for a year or two,' Ted told me. 'I'll find a job with more money, then I can save up. Mum needs my help, so I can't save on what I earn.' I knew that. Even the two pounds he was paid for shows usually went to Martha, plus most of his salary.

The rain stopped; we went on our way, happily planning our future. We wished that we could go on walking and talking together for longer, but we had to go home.

On our return, we embarked upon a new venture: mental telepathy. It was all done by code signalling. A code could be bought from a magic shop in London, but it was very expensive, so Ted devised ours.

We went hostelling again and learned the code as we walked. In the evenings we tried it out at the hostels, where wardens and ramblers were always glad of a bit of entertainment. It went down very well, so, when we got home, we took mental telepathy on stage as a part of the magic show.

Never had I imagined that I would one day find myself doing the La Celeste performance that had so amazed and enthralled me during my childhood wanderings round Blackpool's Pleasure Beach. But now there I was, sitting blindfolded on stage with a crystal ball before me. Identifying articles held up by members of the audience was fairly easy because we had a pre-set code for the usual things proffered, such as the combs, keys, purses, diaries etc. that people always carried in their pockets or handbags. Numbers on notes and dates on coins were more difficult and required a great deal of concentration on the numbers code. But we'd practised hard, so I always managed to get it right.

Crystal ball gazing was nothing more than sleight of hand – Ted's. He asked a few members of the audience to write down words on scraps of paper, which he collected and burned before their eyes. They were switched substitutes. He dropped the real ones behind my crystal ball. I surreptitiously read them as I gazed into my crystal and astonished the audience by revealing each word on the 'destroyed' papers. You couldn't get away with it now, but audiences were naively unsophisticated in those days of pre-television entertainment.

Mind you, crystal ball gazing could cause problems. After we'd done our mental telepathy act at a dinner in Manchester, several elderly ladies came backstage and asked me to use my mystical powers to contact their dear departed. Ted and I hastily departed with the excuse of a last bus to catch.

Chapter 18

In September 1946, Ted was offered the post of assistant chemist with a cement manufacturer in Gravesend, Kent. Heavy industry companies paid higher salaries than Ted got at the textile research establishment, so he accepted the chance to earn more money. 'It means that we won't have to wait for too long to be married,' he told me. So, although we didn't want to be separated, it was the only thing to do.

I sadly waved him off at the station in Manchester. Christmas, when he would come home, seemed years away. But the letters we wrote to each other every day were a great comfort during those long, lonely weeks.

Ted had asked his mother to look after me and she certainly did her best. On Saturday evenings we went to the first house show at the cinema, then, when we got back, she fried battered potato scallops for our supper. During the week, when I was feeling lonely, I often went to see Martha; she always made me very welcome. Before long we became close enough to tell each other our troubles.

Her current worry was, as always, about money. Ted's sister Doris was very clever; when she'd got a place at Manchester University, Martha had insisted that she must go. So off she went, travelling in each day. Bus fares had to be found, but the main worry was the fees for the first year's course, now due to be paid (there were no grants).

Tom wasn't worried. When I was washing up in the kitchen, I heard Martha ask him how she was going to pay the fees. He told her, 'If I have a win on t' dogs, I'll gie thee a few quid.'

'But if you don't win, what'll I do?'

'Oh, you'll manage.' He grinned cheerfully and sat down with his pipe and Saturday's racing programme.

Despite her own worries, Martha showed concern for me. Ted had told her something of my unsatisfactory home life, so she supported and comforted me. One day, when I arrived tearful and furious after a row with Mother, Martha said, 'Never mind, if you and our Ted get married, you'll be all right with him.'

I gave her my sympathy when she told me how she felt about her husband. 'Tom's always been selfish,' she said bitterly. 'I tried to make him change his ways, but he wouldn't listen. He said I should be grateful he didn't bother with other women like some men did.' And that was supposed to make Martha content with her lot!

But she insisted that her difficulties were her own fault because she'd married Tom against the advice of her parents and friends. 'I was told and told again what I'd get if I married him, but I took no notice.'

I asked, 'If you had known what you know now, would you have married him?'

She thought for a few moments. 'P'raps I would and p'raps I wouldn't. But one thing I do know; if some folks had kept their mouths shut, I might have given it a bit more thought.'

Well, when one is young and in love, opposition certainly fuels determination to ignore unwelcome advice, so who can blame poor Martha? I certainly didn't. But I remembered what she'd said; in later years there were times when, despite the urge to warn and predict disappointment, I kept my mouth shut.

Now that Ted was away, he couldn't carry on his annual sale of Christmas cards and calendars from a catalogue of samples. Naturally he didn't want to lose his profitable sideline, so Martha and I took it on. We took orders from regular customers; when the goods arrived we distributed them and collected the cash, which Martha kept in the kitchen cupboard, ready for Ted's return.

He came home at last and we had a joyful reunion. On Christmas Eve we sat happily on the settee in the front room where Martha had lit the ancient gas fire, so that we could have some time on our own. We hugged each other ecstatically, then, much to my surprise, Ted said, 'I wrote to your dad and got his permission for us to be engaged.'

'Wow!' was all I managed to get out.

'You're sure you still want to…?'

'Of course I do.'

He gave me a ring with a cluster of three diamonds. I had no idea that it was not the ring he'd planned to give me, or that the stones were not real diamonds. Indeed, I would have been just as delighted with a ring out of a lucky bag.

It was many years later, after Martha died, that I discovered what had happened. After the funeral, Doris presented me with Martha's pretty diamond and sapphire engagement ring. 'Mother said you were to have this.'

'No!' I stared in amazement. 'It must go to you.' She shook her head and gave the ring to Ted. Later I asked him why Martha had left her ring to me instead of to Doris. It was a sad story that he told me.

The Christmas card money in the cupboard had been intended to supplement a small sum that Ted had saved to buy me a ring. But, when he got home, the cupboard was bare. You can guess what had happened. In desperation, poor Martha had taken the money to pay Doris's overdue fees.

It must have been terrible for both Martha and Ted. 'It was the first time she'd seen me cry,' he said. His grief and disappointment had gutted Martha. She'd felt guilty and wished with all her heart that she hadn't taken the money. I said, 'What else could she have done?'

He nodded agreement. 'Her ring was the only thing she'd got to give; she wanted to put things right, so said she would leave her ring to you, and it was to be yours for always, just as if I had given it to you.'

So she had left her ring to Ted as well as to me.

I still sorrow for what happened to poor Martha; for what she'd had to do and the guilt she had suffered.

But on the day Ted and I got engaged, I knew nothing of what had taken place, so no shadows fell across my happiness. Ted must have felt that, after all, the main thing was we were going to be married, so, despite his disappointment, he too was very happy.

His family congratulated us, then we rushed off to my house where we received more good wishes. I proudly displayed my ring and Dad, beaming delightedly, asked when the wedding was to take place. I said, 'September.' We could have set an Easter date, but we wanted more time to save up. I hadn't managed to save much out of my spending money, but I hoped to find a way of earning extra cash.

Christmas passed in a happy whirl. On Boxing Day, we did two shows on the trot at Sunday school Christmas parties. The following day, the customary meeting between an engaged couple's parents took place. Tom and Martha came with Ted to our house and all went well. Mother was incredibly charming to the guests. Dad always got on well with everybody. He made quite an impression on Tom who later told me, 'Thy father's a gradely mon.' (a grand man).

The next day, Ted had to go back to work. My heart went with him as the train carried him away from Manchester.

I felt very flat after all the excitement of our engagement and Christmas; but at least I could go to Martha's house. With her, I felt somehow close to Ted.

January 1947 was bitterly cold. It began to snow. Pennine

winters always do their worst, but soon the entire country from north to south was snowbound. It was the severest winter in living memory. Roads were blocked and lanes filled with snow to the hedge tops; transport was at a standstill; railway coal wagons couldn't get through, so there was no fuel for domestic or industrial use; gas and electricity were in short supply. Mills closed down; workers were put on the dole. And still it snowed and snowed.

When household coal supplies ran out, there were coal eggs, made from mixed cement and coal dust. They smouldered in the grate and gave out very little heat; everyone was miserably cold. In icy bedrooms we huddled beneath piled rugs and slept wearing more clothes than we wore during the day. Stone hot water bottles, on which you stubbed your toes, soon went cold and added to the chill.

But, when the sun shone, the now smoke-free valley looked beautiful, with tall mill chimneys rearing starkly black against the sparkling white hills.

In February, Mr Taylor sold his bakery and retired. The new owners had their own staff, so I wasn't required. I was stuck at home all day. Even Mother couldn't find enough jobs to keep me busy; we were soon at loggerheads, mostly because I was fed up and irritable.

With nothing in prospect, except work at the mills when they reopened, I decided that somehow I was going to get out of Rossendale. In the library, I scanned the national newspapers, but I was not qualified to do any of the advertised jobs. I even looked in *The Friend*, a Quaker publication that my parents took because they had become members of the 'Society of Friends' and there it was: just the job for me! An assistant vegetarian cook was required at an international hostel called 'Youth House,' in Camden Town, London. The pay was as much as I'd earned at the bakery; it included bed and board, so I would be able to save most of what I earned. Best of all, Ted and I would be able to meet.

Dad raised no objections; despite its London location, the Quaker connection guaranteed a respectable and safe environment. I applied straight away. I said that I had worked as a cook and was a vegetarian. Well, I was for some of the time. During the War, Mother had registered three of our six ration books as vegetarian; this meant that, instead of three meagre rations of meat, we got huge chunks of cheese (it was a few ounces on ordinary ration books), so we could have potato cheese, or cheese and onion pies. These were far more satisfying than Mother's watery meat stews, which left you feeling even hungrier after you'd eaten them.

Although I could make cheese dishes, I knew absolutely nothing else about vegetarian cookery – but I wasn't going to worry about that.

A letter came by return post inviting me to go for an interview with all expenses paid.

On the appointed day, I got ready to go to the station. Some mainline trains were now running from Manchester, but first I had to get out of the snow-blocked valley.

When I opened the front door, I was confronted by a wall of snow. Dad fetched a spade and cleared a path to the road. A snowplough arrived and sprayed the snow back onto the pavement. I struggled through the heaped up pile and slid downhill to the station; it was deserted and snow covered the lines. A porter appeared. 'There's no trains, luv.'

But I refused to give up; somehow I was going to get to London. I stood freezing, then a snowplough engine came chugging down the line. It stopped. The driver stuck his head out. 'Where are yer going?'

'London.'

'I can tek thee as far as Bury, t' line's clear from there; 'op on.'

I quickly ''opped on' and off we went. I sat on a toolbox and enjoyed the novelty of riding on an engine. Despite its open sides, it wasn't draughty; the heat from the firebox, stoked by a cheerful lad, kept me warm. When we reached Bury I thanked my rescuer, got a train to Manchester and another to Charing Cross. As the train sped towards London, I felt as if I was on a great adventure with a new world waiting to be discovered.

At Charing Cross I went to the buffet for a cup of tea. Suddenly a tall, smiling policeman appeared beside me. 'Can I help you? Where are you going?' I showed him my appointment letter with its 'Youth House' logo and address. He took me to the Camden Town bus stop. I must have looked as if I'd been arrested as I walked beside him, but I was glad of his help and protection; I'd been warned about 'the white slave traffic'. No doubt a part of the officer's job was to protect young people arriving from the north to look for work and somewhere to stay.

I got off the bus opposite a tall Victorian building with a large sign, 'Youth House', above the door. The youngish warden, Leslie, made me very welcome. He was bright-eyed and full of exuberant good humour. His secretary, Pam, was about my age. She too was very friendly.

She showed me round the house. The upper stories were divided into small bedsits with a bathroom and loo on each floor. On the ground floor I saw a large common room, an office and a telephone cubicle. The restaurant, with kitchen and larder, was in the basement. Beth, who was the head cook, greeted me with enthusiasm. She was a lot older than me and seemed very efficient; but she wasn't intimidating. When I admitted that I knew very little about vegetarian cookery she said, 'Don't worry, I'll soon teach you,' as if I'd already been given the job!

Pam took me into the restaurant, where the mostly young residents of both sexes and various nationalities were arriving for the evening meal. There seemed to be a great many of them; a cheerful buzz filled the room as they greeted each other and collected their food from the kitchen hatch. Macaroni cheese with cabbage was followed by a strange jelly called agar-agar which, Pam said, was made from seaweed. And there was dandelion coffee. Ugh!

Whilst we ate, Pam told me how Youth House had been set up by the Quakers. Their aim was to achieve world peace through the promotion of international friendship, so young people of all nations and cultures were encouraged to visit or live in the house, which was run on a democratic system, with decisions made by the residents at house meetings.

After the meal, I was interviewed by Leslie and a few of the older residents. I was very nervous, but it was all very relaxed and friendly. They didn't ask about my cooking experience. Their main concern was whether, if taken on, I would actively support the promotion of international friendship. I was very keen to take part in such a worthy endeavour, so I gave my assurance that I would do all I could to help.

After a short wait in Pam's room, I was recalled and offered the job. I gladly accepted.

I stayed overnight in the room that was to be mine. There was a divan bed with cushions for daytime use, plus a wardrobe, drawers, a bookshelf and – oh luxury – an electric fire!

Back home, I wrote jubilantly to Ted; he was delighted to hear that I would soon be within visiting distance. When I told my girlfriends where I was going, they thought I was mad. Valley girls did not up sticks and go to London.

Dad was very pleased to hear that I would be working for world peace. Martha was glad that Ted and I would be near to each other and able to meet. Despite her unhappy marriage, she hadn't forgotten what it was like to be young and in love.

Dad waved me off on the morning of my return to

Youth House. Mother hadn't bothered to get out of bed to see me on my way, but it didn't seem right to leave without a word, so I stuck my head round the bedroom door and said, 'I'm off, now, bye.'

I couldn't say goodbye to my siblings; Margaret was at a college in Cheshire, where she was training to be a teacher. Edwina and John were at a Quaker boarding school, Ackworth, in Yorkshire. The Society of Friends, with whom my parents were much involved, had awarded Edwina and John bursaries provided for poorer students, without which they certainly could not have gone to a public school. They had been reluctant to go and far from thrilled by their sudden transition from home and friends to a school where other pupils eyed their homemade clothes with disdain.

But I couldn't get away fast enough. Nothing I was leaving behind could compare with what awaited me in London.

Chapter 19

I plunged with enthusiasm into life at Youth House. The day began with breakfast. In the restaurant I set a self-service table with toast, plus muesli and yoghurt, both of which were new to me. Everyone kept their own rations of jam and butter in a cupboard; although the War had ended nearly two years ago, rationing was still in force. We got a one-pound jar of jam per month, and a few ounces of butter and one egg each week. The cheese ration was used for the evening meals. Beth showed me how to make vegetarian dishes such as onion savoury, lentil rissoles and beetroot borsch, and I had mounds of vegetables to prepare. Working with lively Beth was great fun; she took me under her wing and often invited me to her flat for lunch. Although she wasn't a House resident, she was very much a part of the community.

During my first week, I asked Leslie if Ted could stay overnight when he came the following Saturday. 'He's welcome any time,' Leslie assured me and added that, as a staff member's guest, Ted would not have to pay for his room or food.

When he arrived he didn't think much of the food, but that didn't matter; we were so glad to be together. Although he had his own room, we could spend time alone in mine.

Naturally, we took advantage of this hitherto undreamed of opportunity, but only as far as it was safe to go, which wasn't very far. There was no pill in those days. Marriage was six months away and the last thing I wanted was to walk up the aisle with a huge lump proclaiming pregnancy. All girls feared the disgrace of 'having to be married'. Actually, it was usually only a matter of bringing the marriage forward, rather than a 'shotgun wedding' with a reluctant bridegroom compelled to marry the girl. Nevertheless, it was the girl, not the boy, who had to bear the shame.

Ted came every weekend. Meanwhile I gradually got to know my fellow residents, all of whom daily went out to work. In the evenings, groups gathered in the common room and that was where I began to work on friendship promotion, which, Pam had warned me, did not include responding to male requests to do their washing. 'They'll all try it on,' she said. They did, but forewarned is forearmed, so they had to accept that there were limits to friendship.

Some of the residents were British; others came from faraway places such as Turkey, India and Persia. One evening, Roshdi, who came from Egypt, asked me to go for a walk. It was getting dark when we set off along busy Camden Rd. We passed Holloway Prison, where we heard the women inmates shouting and screaming. It was awful! We quickly turned back and went along quiet streets. The moon came out from behind the clouds and shone on empty bomb-damaged houses. Suddenly Roshdi said, 'In my country, when you take a girl for a walk in the moonlight, it is customary to kiss her.' I was taken aback; I wasn't sure how this fitted in with friendship promoting. But I needn't have worried; Roshdi merely gave me a brief, gentle kiss on my cheek, then we returned to the House.

But, as I soon discovered, friendship with some residents could be problematic. It was now that I met some refugees from the pre-war Nazi persecution of the Jews. They were teenagers. As children, they had been brought to England on the Kinder trains organised by the Quakers when it had become clear that the Jews were doomed. Their parents and relations had all disappeared in the Holocaust.

I well remembered the post-war newspaper revelations of what had happened. Now I was seeing the effect of the Jews' destruction on their children. They had no one to whom they really belonged. A safe environment, amongst friendly, caring people, could not make up for what they had lost. They needed to be loved. It could be a desperate need, as was eighteen-year-old Benny's.

Pam warned me never to accept gifts from Benny. He had been stealing from shops so that he could give presents to girls who befriended him. His sad attempts to buy love had been discovered; but Quaker support and an explanation of his circumstances had resulted in compassion, so he was not prosecuted.

Pam's warning was probably the result of her realisation that Benny was focussing on me. He frequently tapped on my door and came in for a chat, and I had done my best to show him that he had a friend in me. But by now he was getting too fond of me. I had to cool it, but I didn't know how. I couldn't just push him away. In the end I consulted Harry. He was middle-aged and a sort of house-father. Quiet and gentle, he listened to other people's troubles and often played his violin for us in the common room. I wondered how he came to be at the House, but I knew that he was Jewish and must have suffered for it, so of course I never asked. Anyway, Harry had a talk with Benny and persuaded him to come to my room only when invited. 'Ask other people to come at the same time,' Harry advised me, so I did. A room full of people gave Benny no opportunity for coming on to me and, at the same time, gave him lots of friendly company.

I still have the card Benny sent me on my wedding day. I often wonder what became of him. Perhaps he found someone to belong to; I hope so.

Not all the problems in the House were caused by need to be loved. One evening, at a House meeting, it was proposed that we invite some German prisoners of war to tea. When the War ended, instead of being repatriated they had been kept in this country to work on war damage repairs. The tea invitation seemed an ideal way of fostering friendship between former enemies; but, before an invitation could be issued, Joe had to be consulted because he hated Germans. He could hardly be blamed for that.

He was a Dutch Jew. During the War he had seen his mother and sisters raped by a mob of German soldiers that had burst into his home, looking for Jews. He had tried to defend his family, but the brutes had held him down, then dragged him away and sent him to work in a German coalmine.

A quiet man who kept very much to himself, he often got up very early and worked in the garden behind the house. No one helped him or seemed to appreciate what he did, so, whenever there was an egg left over from the rations, I made sure Joe got it for his breakfast. His usually sad face would light up with pleasure when I set the egg before him and told him he deserved it.

It may seem odd that something as simple as an egg could give rise to friendship, but it did. Joe sometimes brought me wild flowers gathered on his weekend country rambles beyond the city. Flowers were not all that he brought back. He was passionately fond of nature in all its forms, so he collected all kinds of creatures and kept them in his room. He even had a snake he'd found when gathering mushrooms for House dinner. Our two cockney charladies refused to clean a room inhabited by a snake.

Despite his loathing of Germans, Joe agreed that we should invite the prisoners to tea. Leslie contacted the appropriate authority and a date was set.

Joe made a truly heroic effort. On the day of the tea party, he came into the kitchen with a smile firmly pasted on his face and presented Beth and me with a large basket of luscious strawberries for the Germans' tea. A group of prisoners with their guard arrived; they were just fresh-faced lads who were as friendly to us as we were to them. Joe was still smiling when everyone sat down to tea in the restaurant.

Beth and I were making pots of tea in the kitchen when suddenly we heard uproar in the restaurant. We dashed to the hatch. Joe was on his feet, shouting furiously at the Germans. He lunged towards them with arms flailing and fists punching the air. I ran into the restaurant as several residents grabbed Joe and wrestled him to the ground. 'Get his glasses, Betty,' Harry cried. I snatched them from his face before they got broken in his wild plunging. When at last he lay limp, Harry and Leslie took him to his room and sat with him.

I can only imagine what Joe must have felt as he sat watching the Germans eating his strawberries. Did he feel that he had betrayed his family, sanctioned their rape with strawberries? Did the terrible scene he had witnessed rise up before his eyes and explode him into revenge? He had tried – oh, he had tried – to make his peace with the Germans, but it had all been too much for him.

Later, as we danced with our guests in the common room, Joe appeared. He was smiling, but everyone held their breath; what was he going to do? What he did was amazing. He went round to each of the Germans, shook hands with them and apologised. They responded with grins and friendly back-slaps.

Perhaps Joe had needed to erupt and blast forth suppressed anger at what had happened to his family. After that day, he became more relaxed and sociable. But could he ever forget the past? How could anyone wipe out such memories as his?

Even now, for my generation, the scars of war have not entirely healed. It has been said that those of us who were very young at that time were emotionally raped by the terrible atrocity stories; and we do find it difficult to forget what happened. All the same, it has to be said that some of those who fought on our side in the War were guilty of inhuman acts.

Of course, life at Youth House was not all problems. We were far from being an enclosed community; young people of all nationalities came to Monday night lectures and dances in the common room. We had speakers on a variety of subjects such as art and music, plus people who came to report on their activities in centres set up to help the disadvantaged inhabitants of the East End slums. Someone came looking for volunteers to help build a railway in Yugoslavia. One of our British residents went.

One evening, our Joe gave an illustrated talk on 'edible mushrooms'. He was in a bit of a state at that time because his snake had disappeared. It was probably non-venomous, but it was still a snake. We daren't tell the charladies that it was on the loose and we were all on nervous snake-watch, keeping a wary eye open when opening cupboards and drawers. But the snake wasn't found, so we concluded that it had vanished outside. It hadn't.

The day of our spring fair came; it was held to raise money for charity. Ritchie Calder, science editor of the *News Chronicle*, was coming to open the fair. I spent the morning helping to set up the stalls with various goods contributed by London Quakers, then I went upstairs to run a bath.

I was lying peacefully soaking in the bath when a movement in the corner of the ceiling caught my eye. Joe's snake was gliding down a pipe that went through a hole in the ceiling! With a yell, I leapt out of the bath, grabbed my towel, fled towards my room and almost cannoned into Leslie, who was showing our guest speaker round the house.

Ritchie Calder must have thought he'd come to a madhouse when a half-naked form, screeching about a snake, hurtled past.

Joe caught his snake in a flowered chamber pot from the white elephant stall. The fair was opened; many people came and all went well. Afterwards, Joe was persuaded to take his snake to Regents Park Zoo, where he visited it every Saturday. I once went with him; we sat in the park and enjoyed the glorious avenue of cherry blossom trees that, a gardener told us, had been planted long ago as a birthday gift from a wealthy man to the lady he loved.

On my days off, I roamed for miles taking in the Houses of Parliament, Buckingham Palace, Westminster Abbey and the Tower. It seemed incredible that I was actually seeing the famous places I had seen only on cinema news reels. I was totally happy and filled with an exhilarating sense of freedom in my new life, far away from Rossendale and parental control. Nor did I miss a home in which I had always felt that I had no real right to be. Now I was wholly accepted in the family community of Youth House, and Ted I were together every weekend.

Before long, I was introduced to London's theatres. Leslie arranged group bookings for the residents. We saw plays and musicals including *Oklahoma*, a colourful production that burst upon drab post-war London and set everyone singing its romantic songs. Best of all was the ballet, *Sleeping Beauty*, at Covent Garden. It was the first time I had seen a ballet. I sat entranced by Tchaikovsky's music and Margo Fonteyn's ethereal dancing. From that night on, I was completely hooked. I often joined the queue at the theatre's side door, where you paid only half-a-crown for a seat in the gods. The steward was almost mown down when he opened the door and everyone charged up and up flights of stairs in a mad rush to get a seat at the front. The seats were backless benches. 'Move up! Move up!' the steward cried, until we were packed like sardines. Nobody minded; the ballet was the thing. The evening-dressed patrons in the stalls far below couldn't have enjoyed the performance more than the impecunious balletomanes perched high above in the gods.

Sometimes, my closest friend at the House went with me to the ballet. Margaret, a shy, lonely girl, had recently lost her mother and was no longer welcome at home by her stepfather. She had a job hand-painting buttons, but it didn't last for long; she was sacked because she couldn't paint buttons fast enough to satisfy her employer. One of our residents, Rosamund, got Margaret taken on as an usherette at the cinema where she worked. We all helped each other in any way we could; Margaret perked up amazingly now that she had a job she enjoyed and a home with caring friends.

Rosamund, or Roz as we called her, had come from Yorkshire with high hopes of becoming a professional singer. Her singing lessons cost nearly as much as she earned, so she was hard up. She was thrilled when she got her first professional engagement to sing at Toynbee Hall, but in despair because she hadn't got a decent dress to wear. I had recently bought myself a glamorous red dress; Roz wore it for her debut. Swapping and lending clothes was something we all did.

I got on with extending friendship to visitors who came to lectures and dances in the common room. I liked the jolly Jamaicans, who loved to dance as much as I did, so friendly relations were soon established. There were Nigerian law students, too. Most of them were very nice, but a couple of them, the sons of tribal chiefs, tended to be arrogant.

At first the Nigerians had been something of a shock for me because they were so black. In those days our present multi-race society was a long way off. Post-war immigration was a trickle compared to the large numbers arriving later, so, before coming to London, I had never seen a coloured person. But I had quickly got used to black faces and now they were just a part of the scene.

But I have to admit that I found the arrogant types hard to like, especially Earl. Of course, it is easy to be friendly towards people you like, but if I didn't like them, I still had to make an effort because I was committed to international friendship. So, when Earl asked me to meet his ex-headmaster who had come to London from Nigeria, I agreed to go.

We went to a posh hotel in Mayfair. I was introduced to the headmaster, who took us to the dining room for lunch. I had never seen such splendour. The tables were all white napery, silver cutlery and sparkling glass. Assiduous waiters showed us to a table. A menu was handed to me. Oh heck! It was all in French. I thought fast, handed the menu to Earl, asked him to order for me and hoped it would be meat. We never got meat at our vegetarian house, so the chance to eat it was welcome. It was chops with a little white frill on each one; I can't remember the rest of what I ate.

I was not impressed by the headmaster; he treated the waiters with superior disdain, snapping his fingers for attention and flicking them away with his hand when they asked whether something or other was required. He was polite to me, but I felt uneasily aware that something about me being there was not quite right. I was not included in the conversation; they practically ignored me, so I wondered why on earth Earl had asked me to come.

I found out why when I returned to the House and told Pam what had happened. She laughed. 'You were taken along to impress the headmaster; he would assume that you are Earl's girl.' She told me that for some Nigerians a white girl was a kind of trophy to be paraded before friends and slept with. She also warned me to keep clear of Earl. 'He's got two white girls pregnant and refused to marry either of them. He said his parents would not permit him to marry.'

It was difficult to keep clear of Earl; he kept pestering me to go out with him and even left roses on my bed when I was out. In the end I told him, 'I can't go out with you because I am engaged to be married.'

'To a white boy, of course,' he said bitterly. I supposed he was implying that I was racist. I was appalled; I didn't want anyone to think that of me.

Of course there is racism now, but inter-race relationships and marriage are acceptable by many people; in the 1940s they were not tolerated.

In 1948, African Seretse Khama, who became the wise and prudent president of Botswana, tangled with the British over his marriage to white Londoner Ruth Williams. There was a tremendous to-do, with newspaper headlines fuelling the furore. Both the marriage and the presidency were a great success. I remember seeing the couple at Youth House, when they came to lectures, prior to their marriage.

So, in that racist climate, Earl had every reason to feel bitter about my dismissal of him; although I had certainly never intended to make him feel inferior to a white boy.

I felt ashamed of my failure to remain friends with Earl, who now totally ignored me. I was determined to do better in future and avoid giving offence, so, when a friendly Nigerian called Ed asked me to go dancing with him at the colonial club, I went. But I blew it.

I had no idea what a colonial club was. I expected it to be an ordinary dance hall. It turned out to be a totally alien environment, or so it seemed to me when I found myself jitterbugging with Ed surrounded by hundreds of furiously jiving, sweating black men. Suddenly I realised that mine was the only white face there. Fear rose in me. I was isolated in what seemed a threatening situation. I panicked and ran.

Ed followed me outside. He was baffled by my action and my insistence that I must go back to the House.

What I had done was unlikely to result in continued friendly relations. I expected that, like Earl, Ed would now ignore me; but he was as friendly to me as he had always been.

At least I now knew that working for world peace through friendship was not as easy as I had thought it would be: there was far more to it than just being nice to people.

Chapter 20

Summer came in with a prolonged heat wave. Everyone sweltered in the unrelenting high temperatures. There was no relief at night and it was difficult to sleep. With a group of residents, I often walked at midnight on Hampstead Heath; then we took to sleeping in the garden behind the house with our mattresses arranged in a circle on the grass. One morning I woke up with a pair of hairy legs clad in shorts before my eyes. The legs were Joe's; unable to sleep, he'd decided to get up and do a spot of border weeding.

By now, Ted and I were making arrangements for our marriage on 3 September, the fourth anniversary of our first date. First we went to the local town hall to get a consent form; as a minor, I had to have my father's permission to marry. He signed and returned the form and Ted wrote to the minister of my church to book the date, etc.

I had already asked our sisters, Edwina and Doris to be my bridesmaids. It was to be a low-cost wedding, so we were to wear simple dresses that could be worn afterwards: pink for the bridesmaids and blue for me, with brown hats and shoes for each of us.

The purchase of my wedding ring was a memorable occasion. We went to an emporium on Oxford Street, where we were escorted by a floor-walker to the jewellery department and seated on green and gold chairs.

I was very impressed by the beautifully presented scenario in which romance and happy marriage were combined. On the counter, a bowl of red roses glowed beside a photograph of a middle-aged lady whose attractive appearance was perfectly complimented by the sales assistant's mature good looks and silver-grey hair. Like the floor-walker, he wore formal morning dress with a red rose buttonhole. His friendly relaxed manner as he set out trays of rings encouraged me to ask about the lady's photo. He said, 'She's my wife,' and added that they'd been happily married for many years.

Despite the elegance of the establishment, there were prices to suit all pockets. I chose a not-too-expensive ring etched with a diamond design. It was put in a small gold and white box; then the salesman shook hands with us, wished us a happy future and presented me with a rose from the bowl.

We floated out on cloud nine and went to a Lyons Corner House for lunch. At the self-service counter, we were still so cloud-wrapped that we put custard instead of parsley sauce on our fish cakes. Fortunately, the till assistant spotted our mistake and replaced the fish cakes.

Ted had been transferred from Gravesend to a cement works in Sittingbourne, Kent, so he was searching the area for somewhere for us to live after our marriage. It was extremely difficult. With the return of thousands of men after the War and marriages galore, there was a great demand for rented accommodation. Many properties had been destroyed during the War and house-building had not restarted, so most couples had to move in with their families – not an option for us because we'd be living in Kent. Ted managed to find space for us in a cottage with an elderly lady, who agreed to let us have a bedroom and the use of her kitchen. We'd have to share her living room, but we were very lucky to have a home to go to.

My job in the kitchen was coming to an end, but I wasn't

leaving Beth to cope on her own – Roz was going to take over from me. My wage was more than she earned as an usherette, and she would have free bed and board.

On the evening before my departure, I gave a farewell party in the common room. Beth and I had made sandwiches and baked buns and tarts and Joe, bless him, brought a large cream sponge.

I was escorted to the common room by the residents, with Harry leading the way and playing 'Here Comes the Bride', on his violin. We danced and I was showered with good wishes. It was a wonderful evening. Of course, I was sad to have to say goodbye to all my friends. My stay at Youth House had been a great experience – the best time of my life – but now I was ready to move on with Ted.

The next morning he came to collect me. We caught the long-distance coach from London to Manchester. It was much cheaper than rail travel, but took twice as long. The journey seemed interminable. In addition, I felt very tired and there was a nagging pain that I'd had on and off for some time in my left side.

In Manchester, we climbed off the coach and stood waiting for the local bus service to Rossendale.

'Hello!' Ted's sister Doris said, joining us; she was on her way home from the University. She smiled happily. 'All ready for the great day?'

'Not quite,' I said. 'I've still got to buy my dress and a hat.'

'I've got a pink dress,' she said, 'and Mum's made our hats out of felt flowers and net. They're really pretty.'

I was appalled. I'd said we were to have plain brown hats. I could imagine how Martha's concoctions would look, perched incongruously on our heads. They just wouldn't go with simple-style dresses.

I had never gone along with Martha's out-of-date ideas about clothes; but Doris had always worn, or not worn, whatever her mother decreed. She had never been allowed to wear slacks, or paint her legs with diluted gravy browning instead of stockings, as most girls did when clothing coupons ran out. And in Martha's view, low-heeled shoes were not what ladies wore; so Doris must have been the only person to have climbed Derbyshire's Kinder Scout wearing high-heeled court shoes. As she had always done as she was told, I wasn't surprised by her acceptance of Martha's 'pretty' hats, but I was not Doris.

'I don't want—' I began. Just then the bus arrived and cut me off.

For the rest of the way home, I sat and worried about the felt-flower hats. I was in a quandary. Martha was doing her best to help me and save the cost of bought hats. I certainly didn't want to upset her by rejecting her hats, so what was I to do?

When I got home, it was good to see Dad again and Mother seemed quite pleased to see me. There were only a few days left before the wedding on Saturday, but I didn't want to talk about the arrangements. I felt tired out and the pain in my side had got worse, so I soon said goodnight and went to bed.

The next morning the pain was still there. I felt too exhausted to get out of bed, but I dragged myself up. I had to go shopping for my dress, shoes and hat; I told myself that no way was I going to wear Martha's felt flowers.

At the end of the summer season there wasn't much choice left in the dress shops, but I felt too ill to care. I found a turquoise dress that would have to do. I could go no further. My hat and shoes would have to wait. I went home and I collapsed into bed.

Mother came upstairs with a cup of tea and found me crying. 'What's the matter?' Her face went taut as a reason for my distress suddenly hit her. 'Don't you want to get married?'

'Yes,' I wept, 'but I feel so ill.' She called Dad. He took my temperature and sent for Dr Lees, who came straight away. He was probably on red alert due to an outbreak of polio. He examined me, told Mother that I must have lost a lot of weight and asked what I'd been doing.

'Working in London,' she said. He humphed and said that city life hadn't done me any good.

I don't remember his diagnosis, but I hadn't got polio. Mother told him that I was to be married on Saturday. He shook his head. 'I'm afraid you'll have to postpone the wedding.'

Dad went to tell Ted and his family that I was ill, so the wedding was off until I recovered. Ted came. Dismayed and worried, he sat beside me but I felt too ill to talk. I just wanted to be left alone. Youth Club friends came to visit, but I didn't want to see anybody.

I had little idea of what was going on, but the minister of our church must have been notified, and various relatives informed of the postponement. On what should have been my wedding day, I lay in bed, tossing feverishly, whilst downstairs wedding cards and telegrams from Blackpool relatives and Youth House friends were arriving.

Then one of Mother's friends, Suzie, who'd been a nurse, came and took over. She reorganised our sleeping arrangements and moved me into the double bed in my sister's room, and she gave me bed baths. It was such a relief to have my hot, sticky body cooled and refreshed, my wrinkled nightdress and sheets changed. I was very grateful indeed.

Dr Lees came back and put me on a new drug; I think it was called M&B. This, plus Suzie's expert nursing, worked wonders. A couple of days later I was downstairs and feeling fine. Ted was delighted and relieved.

A new date was set for the wedding and arrangements reinstated. Ted ordered taxis and flowers and Dad booked a lunch at a café. He even went out and bought my hat and shoes because he feared that plodding around shops might cause me to have a relapse.

I felt perfectly well, but I was still worrying about Martha's felt-flower hats. In the end I told Ted, 'I don't want those hats your mum's made, but I don't want to upset her. What shall I do?'

He said, 'I'll have a word with Mum.'

I don't know what he said to Martha, but the felt flowers were put away and Doris got a brown hat. I hoped that Martha wasn't annoyed; but I was heartily thankful that my bridesmaids and I would not go down to posterity in family photograph albums with felt flowers on our heads.

Chapter 21

The sun was shining when I awoke on my wedding day. Dad came in to check that I was all right. Mother brought me breakfast in bed and presented me with a set of underwear she'd made for me, plus a short-sleeved jumper of her own for me to wear beneath my dress. 'It'll keep you warm in that chilly church,' she said.

I was overwhelmed by her concern for me. (Although we had been unable to live peaceably together under the same roof, after my marriage we gradually established a friendly relationship and there were no more rows.)

I got dressed. Dad's choice of light brown shoes and hat went very well with my turquoise dress, which, with my spray of pink carnations and fern, seemed much better than it had done when I bought it. Edwina, pretty as a picture in her pink dress, helped me to arrange my hair so that it curled round my hat. Fortunately, she and John were still at home as their Ackworth school term hadn't started, but Margaret wasn't there: she'd gone back to college.

I went downstairs. Mother assured me that I looked very nice and produced the wedding cards and telegrams she'd put away. I was opening them when a taxi driver arrived and dumped a small parcel on the table. He said, 'I'll be back shortly,' and disappeared.

Everyone crowded round the table to see what was in the parcel. I opened it; inside were Ted's pyjamas. Was my face red! Then John innocently said, 'Is Ted sleeping here tonight? There won't be much room.'

The fact was that, on the day after the wedding – Sunday – Ted and I had to return south in time for him to start work on Monday, so our honeymoon in the Lakes had been cancelled.

Mother had asked me where we were going to sleep on our wedding night. Highly embarrassed, I didn't know what to say, so I muttered, 'Ted can sleep at his house and I'll sleep at home.'

Mother said, 'You can't do that; you'll be married. You'd better both come here.'

The arrival of Ted's pyjamas had made me even more embarrassed; I took my red face upstairs and waited for the taxi.

It was a simple wedding with just our immediate families and a few local relatives present. Cliff, home for the day from his holiday in Blackpool, was Ted's best man.

The organ struck up with 'Here Comes the Bride', as Dad took me down the aisle to where Ted was waiting; he looked at me with his heart in his eyes. After a hymn, 'Lead Us, Heavenly Father, Lead Us', we made our vows. In the vestry I signed the marriage register and was given the marriage certificate. Dad kissed me and said, 'God bless you.' Then the organ pealed out 'The Wedding March' as Ted and I went arm-in-arm down the aisle.

Cliff took photographs outside the church. Taxis ferried the wedding group to a photographer's studio and afterwards to the café.

Whilst we waited for the guests to arrive, the manageress showed us the pretty wedding cake chosen by Dad. It was in the shape of a horseshoe, with silver ornaments and turquoise silk tassels to match my dress. And, although he was strictly teetotal, Dad had provided sherry for the toasts.

After the ham salad and apple tart meal, Dad spoke a warm tribute to Ted's achievements, which greatly pleased

Martha and Tom. Cliff made an amusing speech and proposed the toasts. Ted and I cut the cake and Dad issued the customary invitation to tea at the bride's house. This gave both families the opportunity to mingle and see the wedding presents.

The first thing I did when we arrived back home was to thank Dad for making my wedding day perfect; he had indeed done well to carry out arrangements that were normally made by the bride's mother. He'd done it all because Mother had got into a fraught flummox at the prospect of organising a wedding.

Everyone admired our wedding gifts. Dad had promised us a carpet when we got our own home. From Martha and Tom there was a rosebud china tea set. Uncle Lennie had sent a blue and white Worcester china tea set and there were towels, pillow cases and sheets from various relatives. We were also the final recipients of a canteen of cutlery that Ted's granddad, William Henry, habitually gave to any family member celebrating an engagement or twenty-first birthday, then took it back to keep, as he said, 'Until you've got a home to put it in.' Martha had decided that William Henry wasn't going to get away with that any more and told him, 'That cutlery is going for good.'

Whilst everyone talked, Ted and I cut and boxed the small pieces of wedding cake that were traditionally sent to relatives and friends unable to be present at the wedding, or as a means of notification that a marriage had taken place. I set aside a big chunk for kind Suzie, who'd nursed me during my illness.

Our two families hadn't got a great deal in common so, when conversation flagged after tea, Dad took the guests to a nearby cinema. He had no interest in films; neither had Tom, who, after a visit to a cinema years ago during which Donald Duck cartoons were shown, had said that films were 'nowt but bloody ducks', and never gone again. Dad, unaware of that and probably wondering what on earth he could do for the guests' entertainment, must have decided that the cinema was a good idea.

Off they all went. Ted and I went to the Pavilion cinema in Rawtenstall, where we'd gone on our first date.

Years later, when the film *Meet Me at Dawn* was shown on television, we told our family that we'd seen it on our wedding night. There was a chorus of, 'You went to the pictures on your wedding night! You never!' But we did, and we couldn't have enjoyed ourselves more than we did that evening as we sat in the double courting seat we had occupied on our first date. Afterwards, we walked back to Newchurch, exulting all the way because now we did not have to say goodnight and part as we had so often done after cinema shows in the past.

When we got back, everyone had gone to bed. After we'd had cocoa, I went upstairs to brush my teeth. John was in my former bed in the bathroom; he was wide awake and still wondering where Ted was going to sleep. 'Edwina's in Mother and Dad's room, you are in the other bedroom and I'm in here, so where—?'

I cut him off with, 'Oh, we'll manage,' and did a quick exit.

It was a lovely wedding night. There could be no so-called consummation, because I'd got my period. But we didn't care. We were married at last, so we were utterly content as we lay, holding each other close, in the deep silence of the night. 'Together for always, now,' Ted said blissfully as we drifted off to sleep.

The following day we went to collect Ted's belongings and say goodbye to his family. Then we returned south on the long-distance coach. Cheap travel was one way of saving money for a home of our own. In addition, we knew that we would have to do some careful budgeting because

Martha, as always, was very hard up and needed help. She had been happy for us to marry but, at the same time, fearful that she would lose the financial support Ted had provided, even after he'd left home. So he had assured his mother that, until Doris finished her university course and started work, he would continue to give her his usual support. His salary, £480 annually, was very good pay in those days; I planned to get a job in Sittingbourne, so, as we rode in happy confidence towards our future, we were sure that we could manage.

This turned out to be difficult when, in addition to subsidising Martha, we got a house, a mortgage and hire-purchase instalments on furniture to pay, and a baby on the way. But we did manage.

Of course, in times to come, we were to have our problems; who does not? But as the years went by, fortune often smiled on us. We were, as Rossendale's old folk used to say, 'well-blessed', when babies tumbled regularly into our life. We had two boys and three girls, including twins. Parenting is never all plain sailing, so, when they were growing up, we didn't always get things right, but we tried to give them the security lacking in our own young days.

We all had good times together and I revelled in family life. As well as the love of a caring, devoted husband, I had got what I had always longed to have – a real family.

Eventually they all got married and presented Ted and me with ten lovely grandchildren.

Sadly, after some years of ill-health, Ted died from a heart attack at the age of sixty-seven: stress and diabetes had shortened his life.

He said his last words to me: 'I love you.' A few minutes later, he suddenly collapsed and died in my arms.

Our family circle was too early broken; but I am grateful

for the forty-five years Ted and I had together. I shall always miss him, but I am not alone: I still belong to a close and loving family.

Printed in Great Britain
by Amazon.co.uk, Ltd.,
Marston Gate.